IT STARTS WITH A FISH

A Smorgasbord of Stories from Feeding the Famished

Emily Kemme

LOUDHAILER BOOKS

For the Ladies of The W.T.K. Club,
because they research, read, learn, encourage,
and most of all, listen.

OTHER BOOKS BY EMILY KEMME

Drinking the Knock Water: A New Age Pilgrimage
Arrowhead Publishing, 2017

"We all live with ghosts. . .
Some are those of people who've never been born."

So begins *Drinking the Knock Water: A New Age Pilgrimage*. Loosely based on Chaucer's *Canterbury Tales*, the novel takes on life itself as a pilgrimage. One of life's biggest struggles is fitting in with the rest of the human race, and an aspect of that is having children. It's not meant for everyone and yet, true to Darwinian forces, it's almost expected. Giving birth and then raising a child to maturity is one of the bravest tasks we take on.

Named a Finalist in Chick Lit by the 2017 Next Generation Indie Book Awards, this is a breathtaking novel about family drama and social criticism. With searing honesty, *Drinking the Knock Water* takes readers on an emotional pilgrimage through the relationships that make us who we are.

Other awards: CIPA EVVY (2017)

<u>Reviews</u>

Deeply traumatized after her daughter, Arella, is born dead, fertility counselor Holly Thomas struggles to achieve inner peace. Roger, Holly's supportive husband and a prominent fertility doctor, accepts her grief-induced eccentricities, but his intolerant Christian family resents her and her Jewish roots. When Edward, Roger's brother, openly belittles the Bar Mitzvah of Daniel, Holly's son, tensions escalate, and her whole world threatens to fall apart. To overcome heartbreak and reflect on self-discovery and relationships, Holly and Roger take a group of patients from their clinic on a fertility tour. This tour becomes a spiritual pilgrimage for unrealized truths.

As Holly and Roger take their chosen couples on a fertility tour to England, various colliding elements within the patients' lives emerge, thereby projecting how relationships bless or burden us. Pain becomes a recurrent theme in the novel, neutralized by the healing touch of water as a metaphor. Arella's grave is near water, and the visit to the sacred sites of England serves as ritual cleansing for the characters. Artistically nuanced language and the sincere, soothing tone bring out the true beauty of this literary novel. This is an introspective, gentle novel that illuminates and rejuvenates in the same breath.

--RECOMMENDED--The US Review of Books

Fertility doctors confront the lingering effects of personal and cultural emotional trauma. Holly and Roger Thomas have a stable marriage, fulfilling careers, and a son practicing for his bar mitzvah. Holly insists on throwing a birthday party each year complete with gifts for their stillborn daughter, but Roger doesn't complain. His Catholic brother and sister-in-law, however, find fault with Holly, primarily because she's Jewish. Her religion haunts her, almost as much as the death of her daughter. . .

. . . The author often beautifully depicts Holly's self-doubt as she explores different aspects of overcoming trauma. . . [in a] positive tale of moving forward through unexpected circumstances.

--Kirkus Reviews

Dr. Roger and Holly Thomas run a successful fertility clinic in New York City. Roger tends to the patients' physical needs while Holly ministers to their emotional and psychological ones. The couple cherish the routines of their partnership and their happy marriage as they struggle with the pain of a lost child. Holly continues to throw their daughter birthday parties long after the child's been buried. This painful ritual causes her in-laws to question her sanity and is a source of annual familial strife.

Then the Thomases' son, Daniel, decides to complete his Bar Mitzvah. While Holly was born Jewish and Roger was born Catholic, neither parent practices his or her childhood religion. They've exposed Daniel to both religions for the sake of their families, but neither of them expected him to take it this far. Roger's devoutly Catholic family cannot accept Daniel's sincerity, and harsh words are said at his birthday party. Holly and Roger's resulting fight has surprising and unintended consequences.

All this turmoil takes its toll on the workings of the clinic. The Thomases have hosted something they call the Fertility Tour for over a decade. It's an opportunity for their clients to connect to one another outside of their familiar surroundings. Holly conducts the tour; she chooses the participants, orchestrates ice-breakers, and mediates conflicts. Normally she's a skillful operator, but she's lost her confidence. This year's tour is populated by an odd and ill-matched assortment of individuals. Needless to say, this tour does not run smoothly. Roger and Holly must find a way to reconnect with one another in order to salvage the retreat.

The Thomases deal with people at their most vulnerable. Fertility is closely tied to an individual's identity, and both men and women find it difficult to process the inability to have a child. While Holly and Roger have never encountered problems with conceiving, they have suffered a loss and are sympathetic to thwarted expectations. This closeness to struggle and their ongoing religious turmoil provide the pair with a lot of philosophical ground to cover. Is religion necessary to cope with the vicissitudes of life? Is God responsible?

Drinking the Knock Water *is at heart an exploration of the role religion plays in the life of an individual. Faith in a god can both connect a soul to others and sow discord. In the end, it's up to the reader to decide if faith is essential or composed of empty rituals.*

--Manhattan Book Review

In Search of Sushi Tora
(Arrowhead Publishing 2011)

We all have days when it seems the world as we know it is falling apart. Mouthy teenagers, forgotten cell phones, the pressure of deadlines, . . . Lucy Linfeld, wife, mother and former lawyer, chafes at her husband s demands to present a perfect image to their world in his quest to retain his position as a District Court Judge in a small Western town. They used to be partners, sharing their innermost thoughts as they worked together. When his work takes precedence over family, balance is lost, blurring the entire family's focus.

Told with turns of sparkling wit and biting humor, *In Search of Sushi Tora* evaluates the purpose of marriage, and puts a spin on how we can survive the trials of everyday life.

In Search of Sushi Tora was named a Finalist for First Novel in the 2012 Next Generation Indie Book Awards.

Reviews

When it comes to the future of the family, too many people going in too many directions may quickly prove not a family at all. In Search of Sushi Tora *is a novel following the breakdown of such a family. Lucy Linfield, wife and mother, struggles as she grows distant from her husband and his demands of her. As the family seems to slowly break apart, author Emily Kemme creates a world with riveting characters with problems that may seem all too real to many readers.*

In Search of Sushi Tora *is a choice and much recommended read, not to be overlooked.*
--Midwest Book Review

Sushi Tora *explores the raw, vinegary rice of marriage, and evaluates its purpose. Readers will recognize common trials of life, portrayed in the scholarly novel, as their own. Lawyer educated Lucy, now troubled housewife, and District Judge spouse Barry experience marriage problems. Unique survival solutions are addressed. Noteworthy: The reader self-recognized potpourri of life's common problems are uniquely examined with literary excellence, pictorial adjectives, and metaphorical parallels. Women readers will relate to career vs home support of family and the conflicts. Women will gain insight into overcoming trials of marriage, creating a better life's path for self while answering the question, who am I?*
--Mindquest Review of Books

Emily Kemme's debut novel, In Search of Sushi Tora *is a revealing, insightful look at how one married woman frees herself without leaving her husband. Lucy's wild-ride story is rich with details from attorney Kemme's legal expertise. This one's a page-turner!*
--Lynne Hugo, author of *Last Rights* and *The Unspoken Years*

CONTENTS

INTRODUCTION

My blog, Feeding the Famished, is the seed of a well-fed dinner guest. On a chilly February Saturday night over ten years ago, four of us sat in our library to enjoy dessert, spooning up lemon custard and sipping amber Tokay. That's when my friend Diane suggested I take letter writing more seriously.

"I love it when I receive one of your lengthy emails," she said. "It's like getting your undivided attention; you sharing thoughts and impressions about life with me alone."

When someone makes a personal statement like this, my natural inclination is to blush uncomfortably. But in reality, I was already considering putting my writing *out there*. As a writer, that's what it feels like when you set inhibitions aside and open your skull to the world, allowing others to experience the blackness of thoughts pouring out for all to see.

At the time, I was working on my first novel, *In Search of Sushi Tora*. I knew I had to establish a platform, offering potential readers a guide to who I was. A blog seemed to fit the bill.

I began writing it the next week with a story about the thank-you note I received from Diane.

Feeding the Famished started as a weekly post accompanied by three new recipes. Over the years, its frequency tapered off, dictated by work on novels, and for the past few years, a food column and features stories I write for my local newspaper, the *Greeley Tribune*.

Deadlines for paid work generally triumph over writing the blog; even so, Feeding the Famished has been a steady work of exploration, asking the enduring question: *Who am I?* I guess it's a bit odd, starting to figure out who you are at the age of forty-eight. Growing pains are more often reserved for our teens and twenties. For me, I followed a prescribed path, completing college and law school without any side trips for personal discovery. Four years spent practicing commercial litigation segued into taking care of two kids while running my husband's oncology practice from home. Parts of those years were devoted to making hot chocolate on demand and honing my skills as The Perfect Field Trip Mom.

But since 2011, I have written about cooking, traveling, and raising my then-teenagers, Harrison and Isabelle. I marveled as the kids gradually morphed into adults with social consciences. I wrote about the uniqueness of observing the world from a bicycle seat, and how you can never understand a location well until you smell it. There are stories of dogs, remodeling our homes, food and its grasp on my life, and fundamentally, a scrutiny of who and what comprises a decent human being.

The blog became my journey of self-development and acceptance. My writing evolved and I experimented, allowing myself to unearth who I was — in full view of readers, who often weighed in with their own life observations in the comments. The purpose has always been to share ideas and shine a light outward, illuminating the world for us all to consider together.

The tone of my posts varies. There is humor, there is frustration and despair. Naturally, this voyage of discovery entailed delving into the writing process, particularly the hows and whys of the effort, and its, at times unintended, results. I've puzzled over my children's antics and have, most recently, written about the pain of accepting my daughter's bipolar disorder.

Through it all is a steady drumbeat of philosophical sarcasm, often directed at my husband, Dr. K, who usually dreads, sometimes enjoys, and generally tolerates his role as both meme and target.

Readers have often asked me to compile the blog stories in one place for easier access. Rather than lump them all together as one work, I've selected only a portion, taking this book, *It Starts with a Fish*, as an opportunity to weave a unifying thread of growth out of the blog's fabric. Many stories have been reworked and polished to shine more brightly in spots where the initial language may have obscured a thought I was attempting to communicate.

As I scrolled through years of stories to select what to include, I discovered that fish figured prominently in many of the tales. It may have been inadvertent; it may have been a subliminal acquiescence to an underlying theme. Writing can control you like that.

Fish live in water, a medium often representing unconscious thought. There is an old Celtic tradition in which the Salmon of Knowledge — a myth about a salmon who ate nine hazelnuts after falling into the Well of Wisdom — subsequently lends its wealth of knowledge to whomever eats it. Other cultures credit fish as a symbol of fertility and the life cycle; fish also sustain life, both practically and metaphorically. Living in water, fish are imbued with a mysticism all of their own, a self-mastery and channeling of self-awareness. When we say we are plumbing the depths, it is water we speak of, and the fish — with its ability to sustain its life under water — is viewed as an organism that has fierce independence.

To say that life starts with a fish, we acknowledge that water and fish are life-giving. Care of a fish teaches how to nurture another being outside our selves. We reach out of our mortal bodies to seek finer thoughts and transcendent meaning in everyday actions.

In this anthology, you will find stories about fish and the beginnings of adulthood ('It Starts with a Fish'); acceptance of self through art and connecting with nature ('Enchanted by Mud Season'); balancing life both artistic and real ('The Terrible Twos: When Thing One and Thing Two Battle'); and acceptance of the workings of the world beyond our control ('The Community Tank: A Betta Fish Story'). Water as a life-giving element also figured in the theme of my second novel, *Drinking the Knock Water: A New Age Pilgrimage*.

As I gained self-awareness through writing, I gained strength for voicing political thoughts. In sharing them, I was sustained by acceptance from readers; my ideas were validated as being worthy of discussion. At times, as I became more vocal, the ideas were challenged — this is all part of the process of growth as a writer.

Feeding the Famished, as a blog, continues, a work in progress, evaluating life as I see it roll out.

If you are familiar with my blog, thank you for reading it over the years. If you've just discovered this book, I hope you enjoy the journey.

IT STARTS WITH A FISH

NOVEMBER 6, 2015

In many cultures, fish represent knowledge, wisdom, happiness, or freedom. In others, fish are an emblem of maturity. Taking care of a fish in tank fosters empathy for other living creatures. I believe starting with a fish can teach us how to become decent humans.

The summer I turned thirteen, my Great-Aunt came to visit us from Brazil, bearing gifts and wreathed in an aura of glamour. At sixty-five, her bikini fit flawlessly, she sported red-painted toenails, and consumed cherries by the handful. All the grandma-aged women I knew at the swimming pool were swathed in layers of tailored spandex designed to discreetly cover bulges and bumps. My mother tended toward pale pink polishes, if she wore any at all.

But it was her epicurean attitude toward cherries which underscored that Great-Aunt Millie occupied a different playing field.

Growing up, my sisters and I had been instructed to count out cherries into a bowl. Our allotment was never to exceed ten. Cherries were precious fruit.

Great-Aunt Millie was a fascinating whirlwind of assertive womanhood, and her gift to me was a silver fish pendant with hinged scales that could be waggled to simulate swimming.

"At your age, you are entitled to wear a fish," Millie informed me. "It is a symbol of fertility in Brazil and means you are now a woman."

I wore the pendant faithfully for a year or so, until, tired of explaining its symbolism to peers, and at times enduring ribald jokes because of its undercurrent of meaning, I put it away in my jewelry box. Instead, I sported a peace sign necklace, an adornment that better captured my early-Seventies teen mindset.

But I've often thought about that silver fish and the burgeoning adulthood it represented.

When my daughter moved into her first apartment at age twenty, she promptly acquired a red and orange betta fish.

My first inclination had been to advise that it was more than enough responsibility to take care of a three-room apartment, but I bit back my kernel of wisdom. Burton was a fish. How hard is it to take care of one little fish in a garden-variety fish bowl?

Burton seemed inordinately happy in spite of his limited surroundings.

Whenever I visited, he swam to the front of his bowl, waggling fins and blowing bubbles. We had brief conversations about life-in-the-round, and I quizzed him about the view of the street below from his perch on my daughter's desk.

Fertility and all of its interconnected meanings never entered the conversation, and when my daughter asked me to stop by every day to feed him while she was away on spring break, all I could think was, *Please, don't let the fish die on my watch!*

Burton reliably ate his pellets, contentedly exploring his round confines, and developed gracefully flowing fins and a tail. I enjoyed our brief visits.

He was as close to a grandchild as I wanted for a long time, and that was fine.

Since my daughter was handling the responsibility of fish ownership so well, she decided it was time to acquire a cat.

What she really wanted was a dog, but as a college student, it's difficult to manage the boundless energy of a corgi who must go on walks and have a yard to relieve himself. She realized a cat is the lesser furry evil, one which doesn't seem to mind if its owner isn't home for dinner or stays out late.

I told myself I would like this cat, even though I am not a cat person.

But I also wanted to make sure she helped Burton remain happy and not floating sideways.

Adding another living creature to your life metes out another layer of responsibility, another dollop of detail to melt into life's lasagne.

Excalibur leapt into all our hearts immediately — and how could he not? A bundle of black-and-gray striped energy — who doesn't love a kitten, particularly one with such self-assurance? He looked intensely at me and I scrutinized him back, evaluating the inquisitive green eyes that searched my face for meaning and friendship.

Excalibur dominated my daughter's apartment, three rooms she had carefully made cat-safe.

He leapt from chair to table to couch to floor, raced madly into the kitchen, took a swing through the bedroom, and then he was back again, commanding the living room, managing a gymnastic leap from my lap where I sat on the couch up onto Isabelle's desk where Burton swam. The cat's agility was amazing.

The fish's movements had changed.

Once graceful and lithe, Burton was now agitated and confused, often hiding in the bowl's plastic flora. To protect him, my daughter placed a book over the top of his bowl, leaving enough room for air, and not much room for an inquisitive gray paw.

She called me after a week or so of fish-cat ownership to let me know Burton the betta fish was no longer with us. Burton, wrapped in a Kleenex, was given a quiet funeral in the backyard of her apartment building.

My son Harrison, Isabelle and I attempted to come to terms with the disaster in a three-way text:

Mom: *Does Excalibur look sort of pleased with himself?*

Isabelle: *Smug little bastard*

Harrison: *Wait… Did the cat actually eat the fish?*

Isabelle: *No. But he probably killed him with angst.*

Mom: *Oh gawd. My heart is bursting for poor, misunderstood Burton. All two brain cells.*

Isabelle: *I loved him lmao*

Mom: *Me, too. He always blew happy bubbles and waggled his fins at me when I said hello to him. Sigh.*

I know Burton was only a fish, easily replaceable, expectedly temporary.

But in the months he spent with us, he had created a space for himself. From his limited confines, he managed to insert himself into conversations with Isabelle, enabling her to broaden her outlook of the world outside her door. With the responsibility of pet ownership, she had taken a step toward adulthood.

Many cultures revere the symbolism of the fish. It represents knowledge or wisdom, creation, happiness, and freedom, to name a few.

I believe a fish can also educate humans to respect life of any sort.

With respect we learn empathy.

That recognition starts with a cold and slimy organism in a bowl that is only capable of conversing with the world around it by waggling its fins in recognition of another organism in its sight.

More empathic learning comes from taking care of the furry, leaping kitten that most likely frightened Burton to death with those intense green eyes and spiky whiskers.

And from there, the world is open to us.

I've forgiven the cat. Maybe it was Burton's time to go.

In the meantime, whenever I enter my daughter's apartment, Excalibur weaves figure eights around my feet in ecstatic greeting. He rolls onto his back, wrapping paws around my shoes, and purrs. This is only the beginning of my visit. Excalibur's 'welcome' performance in the apartment vestibule takes several minutes.

We are getting to know and love one another, this little creature and I; he has been well-trained in what love is.

And there is a new fish on the desk, in a more elaborate tank with a filter that bubbles from its sealed cat-proof lid.

His name is Merlin, and he is sapphire blue. When Excalibur allows it, I walk into the living room to greet the new fish, and am welcomed with bubbles and a waggling of fins.

WHY DON'T THEY STOCK WOOLLY MAMMOTH MEAT AT THE NEW KING SOOPERS?

MARCH 12, 2011

A somewhat true story about shopping, cooking, and eating — because those activities consume a good percentage of my week.

The elephantine King Soopers that recently opened in our town is gargantuan, to be sure, but it doesn't stock woolly mammoth meat.

I know, because a friend looked.

I was certain she would be able to find it. After all, the new store, with an astonishing breadth of 123,000 square feet, is 24,000 square feet larger than any other King's in the state of Colorado and supplies everything from porch furniture to pincushions.

The meat department had beef, lamb, pork, veal, and poultry of various shapes and species, but no mammoth. I can't figure out why not.

Yes, it's true that woollies went extinct 4,000 years ago. And therefore you might think I'm loony, that eating woolly mammoth is a delicacy experienced a while back in human history. You're thinking it was eaten so long ago that cooking implements like roasters, oven mitts, and temperature gauges were a bit less refined than what we home cooks rely upon today.

Because back then, roasting a hunk of woolly (a term of endearment, guaranteed to get the gastric juices flowing) only

9

required a well-tended fire pit and most likely a spit of some sort to hold up the beast. A spear would work well.

In spite of solid science to the contrary, I believe that eating a woolly today isn't all that big of an impossibility.

You see, I grew up on tales told by my father who assured me he had sampled mammoth meat when it was served to commemorate a very special occasion at the American Museum of Natural History.

I think the meal coincided with a rare find of a mastodon so well-preserved in ice that scientists were able to sample the meat. Suffice to say that woolly had been the pièce de résistance at the dinner.

At least, that's what my father told me.

So, when I read that a baby mammoth was found last year in Siberia and was preserved by Chicago's Field Museum, my first thought, naturally, was, "Hey! I wonder if they'll serve a small part of it for special museum patrons?"

My attempts to contact the museum on this subject fell flat, until a work associate, knowing of my quest, shed some light on the Siberian find.

Evidently, there is a collaborative effort between Japanese, Russian, and American scientists to clone a woolly mammoth baby by extracting DNA from the frozen meat and injecting those cells into an African elephant egg.

I think they came up with the idea from Dr. Seuss's *Horton Hatches the Egg*.

It looked promising that I might be able to locate this protein variety at the massive new King Soopers.

So I enlisted my friend Joan to check it out.

You see, the sheer size of the store gives me the willies. I haven't summoned up enough guts to check it out for myself yet.

She too, was concerned about venturing forth on such an expedition with untold consequences, but being a good friend stepped up to the task.

We decided a certain amount of planning was necessary, including equipment outfitting.

First off, she decided to take her GPS. I recommended snow shoes, trekking poles, and an avalanche beacon. Just in case.

Joan thought this was a wise idea, until she began worrying about cell phone coverage.

We agreed it could be spotty, similar to being on trek in Nepal or Antarctica.

Joan seconded this. Her husband had recently returned from an eight-week voyage on a Russian icebreaker in Antarctica, and is well-informed about such things.

But then general panic set in. She couldn't locate the snow shoes and discovered that the walkie talkie batteries were dead, because aren't they always?

I eased her mind, promising that if I didn't hear from her within the hour, I would call 911 and have them send in the St. Bernard rescue team.

Her husband — who had decided to accompany her to ward off polar bears — really liked that idea and asked me to make sure they sent the ones with the little barrel of liquor around their necks.

Off Joan and Phil went, with me anxiously manning the phone for a red alert.

Or icy silence.

In my worry, I noodled over the idea of what woolly mammoth would taste like.

Being ever-connected to a computer, I Googled it, with little luck. Since no one's eaten fresh mammoth for eons, it's an enigma.

I was able to unearth suggestions that it would probably taste like elephant, moose, or other types of game, but all were in agreement that it wouldn't taste like chicken. Many opinions weighted the taste heavily toward elephant, but also pointed out that because eating elephant is illegal, how would you know for sure?

The mammoth I had sent my friends out to hunt was cross-bred with an elephant, so this is a strong possibility.

Which made my worries escalate.

Since elephants never forget, eating one, or its relative, could be fraught with danger.

By eating an elephant, would you then absorb its memory capabilities? Would you develop a symbiotic thought-link to the one you ate? Worst of all, would the rest of the herd remember that you ate one of their family and haunt your dreams in perpetuity?

All these perambulations took my mind off my intrepid friends for a while and I decided that what a mammoth tastes like is moot.

You eat mammoth for the experience. Bottom line: marinate the hell out of it.

After an hour or more of anxious waiting, I called Joan. I was so relieved: she answered her cell after two rings.

"Should I send in the dogs?" I asked. "Are you lost? Stranded? Have you found the mammoth meat?"

I suggested that, given its sheer size, she might have to ask around for help. It might be that they kept it in a special place in cold storage.

Joan said she was fine and told me to call off the dogs. She'd found the ice cream.

It may be some time before we have a chance to have a woolly feast.

LEARNING TO FLY, LEARNING TO LIVE

JULY 29, 2011

I've owned a bicycle for most of my life. Early on, they were for play. But at some point, cycling helped me shed my insecurities, encouraging me to share my writing voice.

Ilearned how to ride a bike over forty years ago. I learned about life last weekend.

A good night's sleep, sturdy food, and encouragement from friends made up the kernel that provided the answer to the bigger question: what we are supposed to be doing as we pedal through life?

After an organized ride this weekend — the Courage Classic, a 150-miler that takes in four Colorado mountain passes over three days — my thinking has been realigned.

Because I pushed, I learned to fly.

It was a 'tune up' of sorts, an opportunity to whittle activities down to one focal point.

I'm not going Spartan on you. There are times when the 'tune ups' I crave are those of excess: spa treatments, an over-the-top gourmet meal, or the option to sleep in until the sunlight begins to irritate me.

This last is accompanied by an eight-track of guilt playing on repeat. If I don't get out of bed, I'll be met with derision from my family, along with a stack of chores jostling one another and silently shouting, "Me first, no, me!"

Bikes have always featured prominently in my life. I can't remember a time when I was without one.

A blue tricycle, the companion of my little sister Michelle's red version, evolved into a series of two-wheelers that marked the passage of time. For me, bicycles are what a growth chart marked onto white painted door molding are to most other kids.

After the trike, there were a series of blue and red Schwinns. Remember those? Do they still make them? My first 'real' bike — it was blue — had coaster brakes on the pedals which operated by pedaling backwards à la Fred Flintstone.

The next version in my velocipedic quest for the best bike was another blue one with three gears. I yearned for this marvel, pestering my parents for its uncertain arrival.

As is typical with parents, they wanted this major upgrade to be a surprise. I foiled that by turning house and garage inside and out to determine if they had given in. With the extreme thoroughness of an eight-year-old, I found the bike tucked behind suitcases in the garage closet.

Feeling like a rat, and confiding as much to my sister Michelle when I told her the bike had been discovered, we decided silence was a virtue best demonstrated by saying nothing.

And yet, knowledge doesn't bring satisfaction.

I spent the weeks until my birthday in agony, waiting for the chance to ride what I had to pretend didn't exist.

That was punishment enough.

After that, there was a regular progression of bikes of increasing size until I stopped growing, reaching a whopping five foot two.

Theoretically, this would end the need for larger bikes.

And yet, there are always bells and whistles. There was a sparkly banana-seated contraption with silver tassels to stream behind me as I rode downhill. I added gears, alternating between red and blue bikes every few years, finally reaching the elevated dream of a real ten-speed with curved handles (a blue one), to take to college.

It remained locked up outside my dorm while instead, I walked everywhere. Walking was faster than trying to locate a bike rack when you only had ten minutes to hoof it across CU-Boulder's extended campus to the next class.

This ten-speed, now rusty and downhearted, joined another sad bike in marriage. The two bikes sat on the sidelines through the grind of two people in grad school.

There were no bikes in our lives until we were sprung on the world, a doctor and lawyer with a bank account no longer funded by parents and student loans.

Early on during Dr. K's internal medicine residency we met a couple who suggested getting acquainted on a bike ride for ice cream.

That was novel idea. In the past, cycling was plotted by destination. Double-dating biking just because it was fun and included a stop for a treat was unusual, but we went with it. The four of us soon discovered the myriad trails that looped Denver, riding for exploration rather than transportation.

And then there were kids. Kids need equipment. First there were trailers that looked like miniature screened-in porches. Next came contraptions to attach to our bikes to drag children in a desperate attempt to teach them the concept of pedaling.

There was also a tandem.

Note to the world: if you remotely like your spouse, don't ever buy a tandem.

Your spouse might be perfectly charming, but sorry, Daisy. A bicycle built for two is a recipe for divorce once the knot is tied. A person is entitled to life, liberty, and the right to pedal at our own speed.

Once the kids finally learned to stay upright on a bike, biking became a sport.

We also added an element of competitiveness. Mileage counts replaced searching for ice cream, although a beer at the end of the ride felt more than earned.

Cycling is the only sport I know of that is self-powered. You go up a hill so you can go down it faster. It's a grimy sport. There's sunscreen, sweat, and road shrapnel.

But it's a sport providing a view of the world, close to the road, close to the sky.

Climbing mountain passes this past weekend, I learned every curve, the meaning of each grind forward. Pedaling uphill at five miles an hour will do that.

You learn the value of paying attention, feeling the road, each crack in the asphalt critically important, each potentially life-threatening. There is a promise: if you lose your focus barreling thirty-six miles an hour downhill on Fremont Pass, that's the end of the ride.

Why put yourself through this?

It boils down to fear. Or as Mark Twain put it: "Courage is resistance to fear, mastery of fear — not absence of fear." [1]

Perhaps this is why the Courage Classic bears its name. The tour is daunting. Day one includes climbs up Battle Mountain, Tennessee Pass and the dreaded eastbound Vail Pass. Day two begins with Swan Mountain Road and ends with the Fremont Pass climb on day three. All told, that's an elevation climb of 10,200 feet over 3 days.

It was a lot of mountain to go up. I was afraid of it. It was the first time I'd ever ridden continuously with such tough conditions.

And yet, it was the most uplifting experience. It is not a professional bike tour. There are families of all age levels, the old, the young, the handicapped and challenged, in any combination you can dream up.

There is intense fellowship and support of a sort I've never experienced on other organized rides. Maybe it's because it's a community experience, intensified over three days. We shared meals together, waited at the end of the course each day for friends to come in, beer in hand, until our group was reunited. We commiserated and laughed in the hot tub as we soothed sore limbs and backs.

I haven't gone to bed so early since I was ten. We were too tired for fine dining or a movie. It wasn't a regret. The days were full enough.

Of the many organized rides, the Courage Classic stands out. It might be the ride's cause: to raise money for children who may never have the chances we have, the opportunity to live fully.

That's a different fear to master.

After coasting down the east side of Vail Pass, I said I wouldn't ever do it again.

But sometime over the weekend, that changed.

I've already started training for next year's tour. I know I need to ride smarter, get more efficient on hill climbs. I am afraid of it. The challenge is immense. But as much as I enjoy flying down mountain passes, I love the opportunity to learn the road.

For this one weekend each year, I look forward to honing my life down to the single purpose of improving myself. It's all in the balance.

---

[1] 1894, *The Tragedy of Pudd'nhead Wilson; And the Comedy Those Extraordinary Twins* by Mark Twain (Samuel L. Clemens), Pudd'nhead Wilson's Calendar, (Epigraph at beginning of chapter 12), Quote Page 155, American Publishing Company, New York.

WHICH IS WORSE? FATE'S FICKLE FOLLIES, OR THE FORCES OF NATURE?

SEPTEMBER 9, 2011

A study of weather patterns, water problems, summed up after a night-time boat trip to see the Statue of Liberty.

A friend of mine had her car broken into recently and her purse was stolen. All totaled, the vandals made off with close to $600 worth of cash and personal property, plus her credit cards.

The car was parked near a church festival where she was volunteering. The worst loss was her green card. Replacing it will take several weeks, an outlay of $470, and half a day spent at the immigration office.

Without it, she cannot go back to Japan to visit her family. She recently returned from a visit home because her mother had suddenly passed away.

Ironic? I prefer to think of it as an example of the butterfly effect.

That term is often utilized as a trope for time travel stories: the protagonist steps on a butterfly and the world veers off its scheduled track onto a tangent that changes the course of human history.

But the original source for the term came from predicting weather.

It was coined by mathematician and meteorologist Edward Lorenz in 1969 to describe the sensitivity of air movement in the atmosphere — one flap of a butterfly's wing can send predicted weather patterns off onto chaotic trajectories.

It Starts with a Fish

Timing is everything and it is nothing. In weather, everything is up to chance.

The fact that weather is notably chaotic is perfectly acceptable to scientists. The fact that it controls life only solidifies the theory.

It works like this: if an orangutan burps in deepest Africa we may see a hurricane that threatens to swamp New York City and swallow Vermont.

According to this scientific theory, this is true even if the last remarkable hurricane to hit New York was in 1938.

It's because weather patterns are considered to be nonlinear systems.

I took a peek at linear versus nonlinear equations, something my kids can do in their sleep, and became dizzy, but was relieved to learn that nonlinear equations aren't always solvable.

I guess that's why it's acceptable to predict an 80 percent chance of rain. Again, orangutans burping, and other assorted bodily functions go into the mix.

This brand of newfangled math to predict how hard the wind is going to blow is relatively new. Being able to tell people they should put on a sweater — advice I'd always thought was reserved for mothers — has been practiced since the Babylonians in 650 BC.

Then there was Aristotle, who took a whack at it with his *Meteorologica* back in the early 300s, predating Benjamin Franklin's *Poor Richard's Almanack* by about two thousand years.

Franklin and his fellow Almanac writer, Robert B. Thomas, (*Old Farmer's Almanac*), partnered solar activity and the tried-and-true method of 'what does it look like outside?'

Thomas's calculations developed in the early 1800s, using astronomy and weather patterns, are such a good determiner of rain-or-shine that the secret formula is hidden in a black metal box under lock and key in Dublin, New Hampshire. His formula is still in use today.

So, it's as clear as day. Weather is predictable. But is it as predictable as human nature?

Back to my friend, she of the stolen purse. Was she an unfortunate victim, the mark of horrible people who disrespect the rights of others, who take advantage of those of us volunteering for the benefit of our fellow men?

Or was she in the butterfly's path?

Was she parked in the wrong place at the right time?

To put this in perspective, we just returned from a long weekend in New York celebrating my cousin's daughter's Bat Mitzvah.

Given recent hurricane patterns along the Eastern Seaboard, the timing was precarious. Probability predicted a Category 3 or higher storm, with talk of sea surges through the tunnels and subways of Lower Manhattan.

We held our breaths through Sunday night and Monday to see what havoc Hurricane Irene might wreak on our travel plans.

We hoped for the best. A Bat Mitzvah requires years of preparation, studying Hebrew, the Torah, cultural traditions, and Jewish laws. The ancient language is difficult to chant because Torah scrolls have no guidelines for pronunciation or tone. It's the kind of thing that's passed down, generation to generation.

By Thursday morning when we boarded our plane to head east, the power was still out all over Westchester County. It was restored later that day.

But having no power for four and a half days wasn't my cousin's biggest concern.

She was obsessed with decorating the boat for her daughter's party. If you jump over all the hurdles for a Bat Mitzvah, you get to have a really big party.

A hotel ballroom wouldn't cut it. The plan was to cruise the Hudson River at night, loop to the Statue of Liberty, and then chug back into Lower Manhattan.

My cousin wasn't fazed by hurricanes, high water, or having no electricity for days. It made her even more determined that the party boat would be all her daughter dreamed of: a sparkly, fish-themed, starfish-strewn extravaganza for 100 people with a timely, yet thankfully not realistic, 'Under the Sea' theme.

Thanks to us, the relatives sweating in the September humidity, along with a large dose of sparkle, the harbor cruiser had been transformed.

The guests boarded the boat down on 23rd and FDR Drive. We chugged out of New York harbor as the sun began to set. The DJ started up the tunes, the pre-teens began dancing, and the bar was open. For those who had worked to get the very air to sparkle, there were fresh breezes and a view.

I never left the upper deck.

There were relatives I hadn't seen for ages. Dr. K snapped pictures, and we laughed and admired the scenery.

The boat floated under the Brooklyn Bridge and almost out to sea. Back to Liberty Island, and then the cruiser stalled its engines.

Lady Liberty at night, close-up, is inspiring. Just past it lies the lower tip of Manhattan — Ground Zero, shimmering valiantly in the twilight.

It reminded me how lucky we were to be there.

Leaning over the railing, savoring the view and the breeze, I thought of others who didn't have the opportunity to live in the United States, pursuing dreams, following the wind, wherever the mathematicians determined it would blow.

My family was lucky. They escaped Nazi Germany and succeeded in a new country. Now Americans, we are as proud of this country as we were of our former one which cast us out.

I stood near the boat's prow and marveled at the rebirth of the Twin Towers, a beacon shining in the night.

My family was reborn here in this country that accepts everyone.

You might even say we're here because a butterfly fluttered its wings.

FINDING ART IN ALL THE WRONG PLACES

OCTOBER 21, 2011

A kid-centric cross-country trip brings with it the realization that we are surrounded by art.

Fall is my favorite time of year to travel to big cities, the ones stuffed full of history. Point me to an art museum and I'll be there. We've visited Athens, Florence, London, Paris, and San Francisco, often in early October. Temperatures are cooler so you won't be kept awake by the on-off cycling of your hotel room's air conditioner. I've never figured out why, but air-conditioners always want to make their presence known, as if to say, "I'm working *for* you, to keep *you* cool and comfortable. Roll over and go back to sleep."

But in the fall, it's neither too hot nor too cold. The sewer smell of those grand cities, supporting millions, is lessened by mercury's dip. The temperature is always just right, Goldilocks.

But for the time being, destinations like these are not on our radar. I still have wanderlust. But over the past couple of years, that urge has been tamped down by the reality of where we are in life. We are the parents of a college student and a college student wannabe. Our current focus lies with their future plans. The renowned pink light of Paris must wait.

Last week, we celebrated the wedding of the daughter of close friends, visited two colleges, and cheered on a cross-country meet in which our son Harrison participated, one that brought together college students from schools over a five-state region. Starting in Colorado, we flew to Minnesota, had lag time in Wisconsin, and are back now in Colorado, a bit breathless, but content.

It Starts with a Fish

It all began with an idea to meet our son in La Crosse, Wisconsin. A distance runner, we'd seen him run college track, but had yet to connect for a cross-country meet. He wanted us to experience a big meet. The energy and dynamics inspire him, especially the excitement generated by all those people running together. Harrison ran cross-country in high school, but college athletics bumps it up another notch. The training is more intense. Running becomes a dominant part of how you pursue your life goals.

We pulled out the map, trying to figure out if there was something else we could shoehorn in while visiting the Midwest. Being with your son is great, but from past experience we knew he'd be with his team for most of the time.

Our daughter Isabelle had applied to a stack of colleges across the United States. First, we could visit one in Colorado, but surely, there must be one near La Crosse? As it happened, one of her top choices was in Minnesota, so off to Minneapolis we flew. It could be a quick tango in both states. There was a relatively short drive between the two, and both kids were happy.

As you might imagine with this sort of week-long itinerary, there's not occasion to pack much more than jeans and comfortable shoes, except for the wedding. Fine dining and art museums are off the table. In addition to tennis shoes, I tossed in a pair of dilapidated loafers that over the years have logged uncounted miles traversing museums and city streets. Sturdy and comfortable, they're the kind of shoe you don't have to apologize for when you stray into a nice restaurant.

Unfortunately, these shoes have also spent time between my collie Mopsy's teeth. As a puppy, she ate through twelve pairs of shoes, a fact that was accepted with resignation every time I walked through the door of our local shoe repair shop. The owner always sighed when she saw me.

"She did it again, huh?" she'd say. My response is always a shrug. How do you respond to this? I don't think, "Yeah, I killed the dog after this last pair," would earn me smiles.

They'd tried really hard to fix my loafers, but Mopsy had chomped her way through the band holding the top together, which I've now learned is what keeps this type of shoe on your feet. While that's what they'll tell you, the penny loafer's strip isn't just there to stuff a penny into. After walking through the Minneapolis airport, dropping a shoe here and there, I gave up and tossed them into a trash can.

Style isn't a big deal in Minnesota, or anytime when you're off on a college visit. You're there to walk the campus and sneakers are just fine. The person who needed to impress anyone was Isabelle. Mom and Dad are best if they're invisible.

The concept of invisibility is layered, not always affecting the sense of sight. With one kid at school in another state, we've become used to it. Cell service is spotty on Harrison's campus in Iowa, and the best method of staying in touch is through text messaging. You're there, but you're not, and while it's a quicker form of communicating than the letters I sent home in the Eighties, instant gratification read on a two-inch screen isn't the same as face-to-face connection.

But the great irony of being uber-connected in the modern world is made starker by the times when you are not.

We'd begun the Minnesota college visit with a late arrival on Wednesday, wanting only to scrounge up dinner and head to bed. I'd been lackadaisical about making hotel reservations, having made the decision to travel there in late August. I learned too late just how unsmart that was. It was family weekend in both college towns, and I'd managed to score the last rooms in town in Northfield, Minnesota, and La Crosse, Wisconsin. We'd have to change rooms on Thursday in Northfield. The family suite, plenty spacious on the first night for the three of us, had been booked for the weekend. I was glad to book a bed for the second night — and anyway — I reasoned with Dr. K after I told him we'd need to switch rooms, Isabelle would be off in the dorms the next night, having a real college experience. How much space would we really need?

After luxuriating in a beautiful room decorated with Midwestern antiques, on the second night Dr. K and I moved to a hotel room labeled a *cozy*, a space formerly known as a hallway. Smaller than the dorm room where Isabelle spent her night being hosted by college kids, this glorified hotel room was one step towards her eventual separation from us, and we began to feel the slow creep of isolation and invisibility. Becoming a fish out of water or a human stuffed into a broom closet will do that.

The next morning, we collected Isabelle from the college and hopped into the rental car, a quirky retro-style Jeep Wrangler which had looked too cute to pass up, particularly after the rental agent offered me the same price as the boring sedan we'd reserved. Nearly three hours later we arrived in La Crosse. Rattled and shell-shocked, we all agreed that the sedate sedan may have been smarter. Our buzzing ears and inability to talk to each other over the road noise had added another layer of isolation.

La Crosse is a small college town, sitting on the prairie's edge where the La Crosse, Black, and Mississippi rivers conjoin. After checking in to the hotel, a chilly wind sweeping down from the bluffs lining the Mississippi hampered our walk along the banks. We gave up and headed across the street from the hotel into downtown to shake off the road miles.

La Crosse is an excellent spot to visit or to go to college if what you're looking for is a drink. I counted twenty-five bars along one square city block alone. The names were tame at first, growing in potential in the search for lost inhibition.

'Library', 'John's Bar', and then 'Who's on First?', segued into 'Animal House' somewhere along my rambles. I was hunting for a shoe store to replace my loafers. Dr. K and Isabelle were off on rambles of their own. The plan to contact Harrison to see if he could slip away for dinner was under discussion via three-way text. He was bunking with his team at a yet-to-be-determined hotel within a fifteen-mile radius. Kids never know what they're doing until five minutes beforehand. And then they'll get in touch.

In modern life, thanks to cell phones, wandering from your family isn't a big deal. A text message away, it's easy to let them know your next step. Unless somebody driving along Highway 53 to the north of La Crosse knocks out a cell tower, wiping out everyone's cell service. Some stranger, probably texting and driving, had the ability to strand me from the rest of my family, who were somewhere across the street.

Time passed, my panic grew, and I did what most reasonable folks do: head to Base Camp, where we all — well-trained in Boy

Scout mentality — had regrouped. Still rattled, Isabelle headed to her room for a much-needed nap. The weight of two school visits in a week, decisions, and eventual separation from us was beginning to weigh on her.

Isolated again and still without cell coverage, Dr. K and I braved the wind and discovered a restaurant not too far from the Mississippi's edge. Appetizers and drinks could replenish our spirits and warm us up, giving us time to figure out where Harrison was.

Across the river from the restaurant was an old trading post, built in 1841. Sipping a martini, I pondered the lives of the explorers and fur traders plying their trade along that river. Their isolation from the world was so much more than we of the non-functioning cell phones could ever have fathomed.

The sun began to set on the Mississippi, whose waters have inspired writers and poets, composers and artists. Rippled by a cold wind, tinged with a pinkish-grey glow that brought to mind a Corot landscape, I realized how we had the remarkable opportunity to experience art firsthand. It wasn't necessary to travel to Paris to view paintings over one hundred years old. The images were here, no differently than they were for Jean-Baptiste-Camille Corot when he observed light play on the waters of the Seine. It wasn't Paris, but we were living in poetry on the banks of the Mississippi.

We eventually linked up with Harrison that weekend. The cell tower was repaired and communications were restored. Injured and unable to race, he jogged the course with the runners, snapping photos for the team. We tagged along with him, following the sunny course.

As for Isabelle, I don't know where she'll end up, which college will pick her, or which one she'll choose. I wonder where I'll be sending her care packages, filled with odds-and-ends that remind her of home, and the shoes she's forgotten to take with her.

WHO IS IT I'M HIDING FROM?

NOVEMBER 25, 2011

A gift of a book, the loss of a friend, and the discovery that dog hair on the rug is no big deal.

I'm a squirrel. When expecting guests, I stuff things away into drawers and cabinets, often never to be found again.

The problem with the habit is not about what is lost. It's about this: why do I hide away evidence of my life? Why do I feel the need to show a pristine front to the world?

With guests soon to arrive, I race around the house, scooping up kids' homework, dirty socks, sports equipment, and schoolwork. Clumps of dog hair are expected, an added bonus of living with two collies. Lassie was beautiful precisely because she had that long fur.

I entertain formally a dozen times a year. Those are the times I hide my life away. Polishing silver, counting plates, and freaking out a bit all comes into play.

Is the image of my house coming into focus?

I tell you this because of my dream of becoming a writer. Stuffing stuff away is the backstory.

I've just finished reading a story published in 1910 by **Richard Harding Davis**, 'The Make-Believe Man,' a short story in the book *Once Upon a Time*.

John, my neighbor several houses ago, gave me the book after I'd confided that my heart's desire was to be a writer. A teacher who wasn't one to push, he suggested I'd enjoy reading it.

At the time of his gift, nearly every minute was consumed by a toddler and a newborn. I was managing Dr. K's medical practice and volunteering for several organizations, too.

In those days, minutes of reading sheared from obligations released me from reality.

Even with Davis's reputation as journalist, wartime correspondent, author, playwright, and great friend of Teddy Roosevelt, *Once Upon a Time* was relatively unknown. I stuck it on the bookshelf, admiring its pretty embossed cover.

Over the years, I've glanced at John's gift. Why was this particular book pivotal to my education if I wanted to be a writer? I sensed that opening the cover and turning its pages were all incremental steps to a new, frightening self.

Instead, I kept the book shut, hiding away its secrets.

A couple years ago I stopped working for Dr. K's practice and began writing.

I still hadn't read Davis's book.

But deciding to become a writer ushered in a more relaxed method of entertaining.

Being a writer entailed a lot of time spent exploring my thoughts and in the process, I became outwardly more relaxed. My mind was busily considering so many more things than silver polish.

The more relaxed I became, the more people we invited for dinner.

Silver polishing was pre-empted by Chinese take-out shared from white boxes, enjoyed by candlelight.

And in tiny ways, I continued to relinquish the hold my house had on me.

Dishes could become clean whether scrubbed at one in the morning or in bright daylight. Dog hair exists, along with the added benefit of sharing hugs with dogs.

The years passed, as did my friend John.

After his funeral, I mustered the courage to open his book.

Even though written over one hundred years ago, Richard Harding Davis's words resonated as if written today. He wrote of people, their sentiments, fears, and desires. His stories were simple, stories of life, with a poignancy that brought me to tears.

'The Make-Believe Man' was a tale of two clerks in New York. One, a charlatan who dressed for adventures of his own creation, presented himself not as he was, hoping to meet the fabulous. The other, a man who acknowledged his upbringing as a fisherman's son, was content to be a clerk for the moment — aspiring to greater things as life unfolded.

Together, they have an unexpected adventure — saving shipwrecked Irish nobility thanks to quick thinking and the fisherman's son's familiarity with the sea.

As I read, a classic fable unrolled: it is better to appear as we are, not as we wish to be. The conceited clerk looked foolish, the one who was down-to-earth offered a lifesaving solution.

As I read, I came to understand that people are people no matter the century.

If I had to choose between camaraderie or cleanliness, I choose the former. Pretending no one lives in my house is futile. It serves no purpose other than to make me crazy.

LET'S THROW A WRENCH INTO THE WORKS: BEST MOM EVER

APRIL 19, 2012

The whole idea of signing up to be The Best Field-Trip Mom Ever is because you want to spend time with your kids — right?

Here's a quiz for you:

Your daughter, a senior in high school, asks if you would mind accompanying her on the Advanced Placement Literature field trip to the big city, incorporating an all-day spin through art galleries, cupcake factories, book stores, art museums, and a play. You will be permitted to eat at scheduled points throughout the day and into the night. Driving a carload of teenagers is required. Sitting down to rest is optional.

Your response is:

(a) I'm tired of letting the dogs in and out all day long and will be taking a lesson in taxidermy that day to remedy the problem;

(b) I need to be home for the lawnmower guy to show him all the spots he missed last week;

(c) Sorry, that day is full to the brim. I have to oversee the septic pump extraction. It's been a few years, so that'll consume my every minute;

(d) OMG! Does this mean that you still recognize me as your mother and would agree to be in the same room with me in front of your classmates? Is it too late for me to say yes? Where do I sign? Does the teacher need my birth certificate?

For the sake of this story, I'm hoping you've opted for choice (d). If not, it's up to you whether you would like to continue reading.

You probably ought to know that I am a field trip veteran and have been ever since Harrison was in pre-school.

I'm not sure if this stems from admiration of my sparkling wit and enjoyable company, or the cold hard fact that we've owned a string of beasts with four wheels. The current version is a Chevy Suburban nicknamed 'The Great White Buffalo'. Its name was acquired *en route* during a previous field trip exploring the wilds of Yellowstone National Park. The vehicle is as large as a mastodon, is white, and I hate it because it's hell on wheels to park.

The nickname 'Great White Elephant' would be more appropriate, except there were no elephants milling around Old Faithful, the place where its name was inspired. Buffaloes are much more run-of-the-mill in the American West.

On a previous voyage with Harrison — in a royal blue Suburban I hated just as much as the GWB — I accompanied three fifth-grade classes, exploring Colorado from end-to-end, logging 1,200 miles.

Sleeping arrangements were primitive, for a JAP (Jewish American Princess) who excels at making reservations in hotels which are unique.

The itinerary included bunking down in middle or high school gymnasiums. Gyms have plenty of elbow room, but my brother-in-law Jerry pointed out that I might have a problem with the special effects.

"Like what," I asked him. "Do they have astronomy shows on the gym ceilings?"

I couldn't remember having light shows in high school, but nowadays, kids are more technologically advanced.

Gymnasiums haven't changed much, my bro-in-law explained. The floors are still glossy wood strips, the team mascot adorns a wall in garish paint, and a lingering essence of stale sweat is a deep-rooted fact.

None of this was a huge problem, I told him.

"You're going to be sleeping in a gym. There's no way to turn off the lights," Jerry said.

This information induced waves of panic. I'm one of those moles who needs blackout curtains to sleep. And as much as I looked forward to traipsing all over Colorado to visit Bent's Fort and Mesa Verde, this was a major problem.

"If I were you," he suggested, "I'd bring a pop-up tent. Then you're covered."

Early the next morning I reported for duty sporting my prized Indiana Jones hat I'd discovered in Disneyland's Adventureland, along with the royal blue Suburban. There was also a tent, air mattress, and a suitcase that weighed sixty pounds. Somewhere in the beast sat the ten-year-old child I had birthed a while back.

Without airline weight restrictions, I packed everything. Trekking through ancient anthropological habitats didn't mean I needed to dispense with fashion.

That week, there were several fathers, also chaperones, who took turns lugging my suitcase and other assorted 'camping' gear. I was given the 'Kitchen Sink' award on that trip.

But I'd decided for Isabelle's trip I could drag my own equipment. This JAP could go camping in gymnasiums and haul her own crap!

I stuffed everything for the Yellowstone trip into an oversized duffle bag. The evening before the trip, as I slung the bag into the back of the soon-to-be-labeled Great White Buffalo, something in my neck cracked.

But I was one tough JAP. I ignored it and went inside to cook dinner.

As dawn broke the next morning, when I tried to get out of bed it felt like someone had driven a Phillips screwdriver into my neck. Wavelets of pain emanated from all five points of an invisible wound, sending searing needles down my spine.

"Can you help me put on my turtleneck?" I asked Dr. K meekly. Suspicious, he asked why.

"Because I can't turn my head to the right."

Have you ever noticed how effective it can be to give a straightforward answer? Mincing words only ends up raising people's hackles.

"That'll be interesting, trying to change lanes in traffic," he said.

"I'll figure it out!" I insisted. "Isabelle is depending on me to be there! She's asked me to go! I can't back out now. Plus," I explained, "I'm driving overflow. They need me to transport five kids. They can't just strap them to the roof of the bus."

He groaned, but stuffed me into my turtleneck and helped me back out of the driveway. Luckily, it was early enough in the morning that I didn't need to turn my head to watch for traffic.

As I pulled up to the school, Père Chestnut, partner in crime and parent of another field trip kid, flagged me down by nearly jumping in front of the beast. Unable to turn my head, I'd nearly missed him standing there on the sidewalk.

"You don't get to ride shotgun," I informed him.

Pouting, Père began to protest. He wouldn't sit in the back seat with the kids, but before his dignity imploded completely, I interrupted.

"You've got to drive the beast; I can't move my head."

We developed a plan. Père Chestnut drove the monster and massaged my neck. Every time he accelerated or braked, I yelped and he panicked.

We were proceeding according to the directions of his chiropractor brother, whom we had dialed in on speakerphone. The massage efforts continued for mile after mile of Colorado highway. His brother hadn't called it *massage*. I think his word for it was *manipulation*, or some such rot.

Hours later and miles into Wyoming, Père Chestnut and I both heard my neck crack.

We looked at each other in astonishment, commenting in simultaneous awe, "Wow." This was interesting in and of itself because I could now pivot my head. Who knew you could hear bones actually realigning? It was astonishing. It was also a shared 'Yuck!' sort of moment.

The sharp pain was gone, replaced by muscle spasms, my body's message that I'd pushed the limit.

Another field trip mom — a practicing doctor — unearthed a miracle drug in her kit, Skelaxin. After a day of popping pale pink pills, I was back in the driver's seat.

That first evening, lying flat on my back in the pop-up tent, unable to turn over, afraid I'd fall off the air mattress into the gym floor's abyss, Isabelle peeked inside the tent flaps.

"I know you're in a lot of pain," she said. "But it means the world to me that you're here."

That had been the last school field trip.

As the kids hit middle school, field trips vanished, replaced with me in a car alone, traipsing around the state so I could cheer them on while they competed in various sports events. Shepherding children through zoos and museums evolved into me sitting on the sidelines watching them perform athletic feats.

Relegated to memory, thoughts of Yellowstone, along with so many others, were held close. I paged through them in my mind at times, believing they were the last.

The invitation to tour art galleries in Denver was an unexpected gift.

And then, it rained.

Rain isn't a problem if the plan is to visit art museums and watch a play.

Rain is an enormous problem if your daughter is scheduled for a tennis match the day before visiting art galleries and watching plays.

That is when an awful 'c' word enters your vocabulary: choose.

An obligation is binding, whether to your tennis team, or to the teacher to whom you'd promised to drive kids to Denver to visit art galleries.

Isabelle went to her rescheduled tennis match. And I drove her classmates on an educational expedition without her. She won her match and did not disappoint teammates. I ventured out in the world, learned new things, and shared the experience with all ages.

Out of disappointment, came novel experience, an opportunity to see the world as imperfect and revel in its flawed beauty.

THE BULLFIGHTER'S GUIDE TO GROCERY STORE ETIQUETTE

MAY 4, 2012

I take a look at the similarities between bullfighting and grocery shopping. Both are art forms in their own right, and what is closer to life and death than filling the refrigerator?

The month of May is the 'done with' month, that time of year when we cross obligations off calendars and look ahead to summer. It's been some time since I walked the halls of higher education in pursuit of knowledge, but that old 'getting out of school' chant has a long half-life.

'No more pencils, no more books, no more teachers'…' well, I know you remember the rest of it, too.

And yet, the pressures of May exist, even if we aren't putting pencil to final exam paper.

Work, family, community: the demands of each peak during this season.

My kids are out of high school now, but back then, much of the seasonal tension was tied to sporting events. For some reason, there was always an out-of-town tennis or track meet on Tuesdays.

As a creature of habit, on Tuesdays I exchange my computer for domestic pursuits. The grocery store and errands fill the morning hours. The laundry room and steam iron occupy me into early evening.

I tell people that Tuesdays are my domestic diva days. Because yes, I iron clothes. Archaic yet soothing, ironing is my Zen time.

This is why Tuesdays, full of obligatory tennis and track meets, raise my blood pressure.

I mean, get real. Whenever housework meets time restraints, anything remotely Zen is replaced by bottled-up tension.

May falls in the zodiac when the Sun crosses the astrological constellation Taurus — the bull — known for aggression. And it was on these Tuesdays in May that I noticed the similarities between bullfighting and grocery shopping. They are both art forms in their own right.

The novelist Ernest Hemingway had an obsession with bullfighting, or what he called 'Tauromania'. In *Death in the Afternoon*, he wrote about the spectacle of life and death in the bullring. Death usually came for the bull, and on occasion, the matador. Hemingway admired the bull arena for this visual opportunity offered to those not faint of heart.

A grocery store on a Tuesday in May is the closest approximation to a bullring I can think of. After all, what is more akin to life and death than filling the refrigerator?

Similar to a bullring, the place where we forage for sustenance (should we decide to cook rather than drive-thru) is a very public forum.

The wire cage of a shopping cart leaves nothing to hide. The world can see exactly how we live and eat. How many times have you cast a roving eye into your aisle-neighbor's cart, scanning, adding up the boxes of frozen pizza and cat food tins? How many times have you been tempted to remark to a fellow shopper, "Yeah, that's right. We don't use corn cobs anymore, either."

As in the bullring, all actions are under exacting scrutiny from the moment I cross the store's gaping threshold.

As a regular, in that I have shopped at this store for over twenty years, the employees are familiar, and I am the matador. All eyes are upon me.

"What is her mood today?" the clerks whisper to each other.

Some of them aren't that subtle. Taking note of manner of dress, shoes, and stride, they comment aloud, "She's on a mission today," if I seem rushed.

Hemingway's prized bullfighters in his novel, *The Sun Also Rises*, similarly had a purposeful mission.

There was a correct way, the artistic way, of holding the cape, working closely to the bull, never faking risk, knowing it was there, showing the danger to the crowd.

Stocking up on provisions requires ritual, method, and passionate emotion in equal measure to bullfighting.

You see, there is a no-fail method to grocery shopping: begin in produce, evaluating specimens minutely, taking care to inspect, prod gently, observe new offerings. There is the possibility that an entire menu may change based on availability of a necessary vegetable. The art form is honed to a sharp edge if the shopper can make substitutions without panic.

Next, head to the deli, evaluating, always.

Then meats, breads, dry goods and so on, until the end, when dairy products are reached.

Then, and only then, can the shopper proceed to checkout, finishing the dance with a smooth flourish.

There are those days, and every matador has them, where the produce is wilted or the desired vegetable cannot be had. Aisles are crowded with fellow matadors, tempers flare, bulls snort and paw the ground. The emotional temperature in the arena rises to boiling point when shelves so crowded with goods fail to yield results because that precise brand of olive oil cannot be located.

This is all part and parcel of the shopping experience, the spectacle, the horror.

If the matador is an *aficionado*, a person with the passion and desire to go home and create a meal, the grocery clerks will forgive all, because they *know* that you are a cook, that you shop at their store out of the pure enjoyment of the activity, that these are the steps which lead to creation.

But there is one thing grocery clerks will never forgive, no matter how much *aficion* is written on your sleeve or piled up in your basket, and that is the cell phone. It is a grievous sin. It is a mark of disengagement with the art form.

On one certain Tuesday in May, as I evaluated where to find an elusive can of diced organic tomatoes without basil leaves, jalapeño peppers, or salt — just plain tomatoes — my cell phone rang.

Engrossed in search for the perfect can of diced tomatoes, I ignored the ring. It was followed by the tweet of a text.

Callers can wait, texters can't. That's my rule and most people needing to reach me *Right now, Mom!* know it.

The text was from my daughter's tennis coach, inquiring whether Isabelle was riding on the team bus.

"Hell yes!" was my immediate thought.

The team had to arrive at the competitor's school an hour before the match began, and this particular school was forty-five minutes away. I hadn't planned to arrive at the school until yellow balls started bouncing over the net.

I didn't want to drive Isabelle. As it was, I was up to my armpits in unpaid groceries which had to be taken home and stored away.

Texts were exchanged, and I learned that Isabelle had missed the team pictures and the bus was leaving in ten minutes.

Panic ensued and I texted Isabelle, who gets high marks in the quick-responder category. She was still in class because the front office hadn't dismissed her.

While creating a flurry of texts, I stormed up and down the grocery store aisles, grabbing foodstuffs off shelves while directing my daughter.

Get out of class, with tennis racquet, and get onto that bus!

But I, ever the skilled matador, remained cool, calm and collected, never raising my voice. A text message is an effective tool, hiding emotion yet conquering the world. You can yell mutely by sending texts.

It was a lengthy, soundless conversation, except for the repeated tweets and blurps of incoming and outgoing messages.

But the silent conversation via cell phone infuriated my checker. She tossed pears down the conveyor belt, toppled bottled water onto fresh flowers, doing anything she could to make me aware of her displeasure.

I apologized between texts, explaining the difficult situation of trying to locate my daughter and get her on that bus. It was a mother's angst that carried no weight. Today, I lacked *aficion*. There was no eye contact, no casual banter, no 'What are you making for dinner this week?' sort of give-and-take.

Without the expected exchange of emotion, I was no longer the swaggering matador in control of the arena. No, I was a dead matador in the grasp of Tauromania.

I prefer days where I go through life like a skilled matador, dealing with horns and hooves with grace and dexterity.

But I know there will be days when Tauromania has me in its grasp. Those are the days when I go home, unpack my groceries, and hide under a rock.

THE BLIND LEADING THE BLIND

MAY 18, 2012

If you're a teenager, there is no good reason for best laid plans.

Back in high school, my mother would ask me what my plans were for the evening. I'd shrug, tell her my friends and I were headed to a game (the sport was season-dependent) and then afterwards, who knew for certain?

She would then instruct me on the importance of finding things to do, that it wasn't a good idea to Just Stay Home.

After wriggling around the topic, I'd eventually explain that our ringleader would come up with the next step.

Every group has one of those, and it wasn't me.

My friend Susan, the one with the vintage, banana-creme convertible, made most of our rules, which we followed without hesitation.

"So, it's the blind leading the blind," my mother always remarked.

Decades later, nothing changes all that much.

My kids' response to a Friday morning query of, "What're you up to for the weekend?" generally earns me a look which says, "Mom, it's way too early to tell. Seriously."

And it's not just the teenagers.

In a recent conversation with my friend Dimitria about whether she and her husband could join us for a concert — one we'd discussed with enthusiasm over a month ago — she said that when she'd called to order tickets, the show was sold out.

Over back-and-forth emails, it unfolded that she had been overwhelmed by life and hadn't gotten her mind wrapped around the need to purchase tickets. It wasn't until there were no tickets left that she decided it would have been a lot of fun.

"We'll do it next time," I reassured her.

Teenagers may be erratic, but adults are equally capable of inconstancy.

When you're a grownup, not knowing what you are doing for the weekend can be relegated to any number of psychological pathologies, be they chronic or simply sporadic occurrences.

While Dimitria admits to a tendency to procrastinate until a crisis situation develops, and then later regrets missing something fun, I am a waffler. I can't make up my mind. Should I stay or should I go? Will I be too tired, and then resent the fact that I'm not at home in my sweats eating leftovers?

Even if I've got tickets, I'm never certain that I'll go to an event. Because, well, you know, those leftovers need to be eaten.

Given our own acknowledged inabilities, Dimitria and I agreed we couldn't be irritated with our offspring's' indecision and uncertainty regarding their own activities.

How can we instruct them to 'Do what I say, not what I do' when we don't always follow through on it?

THE CELL PHONE ALWAYS WHINES

MAY 18, 2012, PART TWO

I'm a wordie. I dare you to autocorrect me, you damned iPhone.

There is only one thing in life about which I am certain. My iPhone is always right, or at least it thinks it is.

Even after I've typed over its autocorrects — because I do know what I want to say — my phone suggests an entirely different word, assuring me I didn't mean what I said.

It's frustrating as all get out.

The algorithmic predictions by word-monkeys crawling over linguistic tendencies on the internet to determine language patterns common to twenty-first-century mini-QWERTY keyboard texters are not indicative of my thoughts and intentions.

What we need instead of word-monkeys is an algorithm to predict human behavior.

I remember a passage in *Gone with the Wind* — that epic tale of a bygone era of slaves, hoop skirts and cotton plantations — where Scarlett O'Hara, volatile protagonist and expertly trained flirt, bemoans the indeterminable nature of Rhett Butler, one of the story's two male enigmas.

Trained by her mother and her Mammy in the art of husband-catching in the Old South, Scarlett understood that men would react in a preordained way if she prompted them with the expected verbiage.

Although I have always wondered what those men (soon-to-be-caught by vanity-engorged feminine wiles) were actually thinking about the silliness of the entire process, it is only in a false society where human behavior can be predicted by algorithmic calculations.

I'll admit that I'm perfectly happy whiling away half an hour checking out the latest mangled language blooper on the *Damn You, Autocorrect!* website. I am also aware this is an exercise in avoidance and procrastination. It's much more fun reading jokes on the internet than banging out this week's blog post, or finishing up writing the next chapter of my new novel. Even so, I think it has less to do with not wanting to get a job done and everything to do with fear of the unknown.

It was at about this point in my mental perambulations on time-wasting and indecision when my daughter Isabelle wandered into my office with the request that I review the speech she'll deliver at next week's high school graduation ceremony.

"It's all about the future," she told me.

Her speech was full of ebullient hope and resolve, that the Class of 2012 would provide answers to solve the world's problems. I didn't want to pop her bubble, because she's wonderful and off to new adventures in the great, wide world. But I believed there was a way to harness her energy and good intentions.

"Let's just admit that we don't know everything but we'll keep on learning and challenging ourselves to figure it all out?" I suggested.

Because face it, every day that we learn something new will only bring benefit to us all.

I don't have many answers, and I believe this is why there is hesitation when my cell phone whines that the word I think I want to use is wrong.

Because there are days when I can't make any decisions at all, except possibly that, yes, I would love to have my coffee this morning.

HITTING THE WINDOW

AUGUST 24, 2012

Getting from point A to point B is one thing, actually seeing the route itself, quite another.

When I was a kid, a lot of our vacations involved traveling around the country by car.

There were a handful of vacations where we flew to our destination. Memories of those are hazy; I'm pretty sure we flew because they required crossing large bodies of water. When I recall family trips growing up, a Ford LTD station wagon with wood on its sides figures prominently.

I suspect my dad's job as a radiologist had something to do with opting for road trips instead of traveling in a cramped airliner. After being cooped up in the dark reading X-rays all day, he yearned for sunlight.

We all had allotted spaces in the station wagon from which we rarely deviated. My parents sat in front, Dad driving and Mom in the passenger seat. My sisters were in the middle, and I was relegated to the 'way way back.' I don't know why we called it that. It's not like a station wagon is as big as a van, or even most SUVs. Nonetheless, that's what we called it.

My sisters were more sociable than I was. They had Barbies and stuffed animals who enjoyed talking to each other, or they would work on coloring books together.

My dad carved out a way way back space for me. Approximately three feet long and a foot or so wide, I cocooned, surrounded by suitcases and a cooler, facing the rear window. I had books and from the teen years onward, a round yellow transistor radio with an earplug, an early version of the iPod, I suppose. Best of all, I had a view of the world as the miles ticked past. I spent a lot of time gazing out the rear window, speculating about the pockets of humanity out there as we zipped past.

For me, a road trip has only positive memories. It's a time to separate from what's familiar, letting the road and unknown factors guide you.

So when our kids were getting ready to head off to college, I wanted to drive them to their destinations. Dr. K was wary of the idea. The oldest, Harrison, went off to Iowa, 780 miles from home. Dr. K opened fire on the topic by suggesting the mailing option — not of the kids — but for their accoutrements, their stuff.

"We can ship everything and then fly them to school," he parried.

"It's only an eleven hour drive each way," was my riposte. "It'll be fun! We can explore the country!"

What I didn't say was how much it meant to me to be cooped up with my family in the Suburban. There would be something special about driving those miles together. I knew we wouldn't see our son until Thanksgiving. Those shared experiences counted for something — taking in the sights, locating lunch stops, bitching about cramped legs, finding the cleanest restroom.

I think Dr. K finally understood what I needed. Into the Burb we piled.

That was three years ago, and I've driven the wind-tunnel corridor of I-80 east a number of times now. We never drive it straight through. I need a measure of civility, which includes feeding me a decent dinner in Omaha, along with a martini or two. Call it joint lubrication to ease sitting in the car for hours on end. Plus, walking from the hotel to dinner in the soft summer night goes a long way towards making a person feel a bit more human.

Just to make life more interesting, Isabelle chose a college in the opposite direction. Ever one to compete with her brother, she increased the mileage as well, up to 1,080 miles away from home.

"Why is it that neither of the kids picks a school in our time zone?" Dr. K mused.

"It'll be fun!" I said, a bit lamely. "It's great family bonding time. We have to figure out how we get there. And we get to explore I-80 in the opposite direction."

Even I will admit my enthusiasm had dimmed.

I've discovered that college transportation excursions are less chock-full of charm, more forced march. We engage in a dedicated rush, getting from point A to point B in record time. Once we arrive on campus, there is unpacking and dorm-decorating to accomplish. The idyllic nature of a road trip — exploring unknown territory — becomes lost, no less than it does when industrial mechanization takes over.

As kids, we used to play the license plate game: whoever spotted the greatest number of plates from different states in an allotted time won. We would also collect car brands. American makes were easiest, but foreign models scored higher.

Now, we just want to beat the clock. Can we best Google Maps' estimate and shave off time?

And I don't think we're the only people who travel from KFC to KFC.

One of our friends, with family in Seattle, employs a divide-and-conquer tactic. She and her husband each purchase a ticket to fly to their destination of choice (either Seattle or Denver). One parent drives their college student westwards to Seattle and flies home to Colorado, the other parent departs from Washington and takes a turn behind the wheel, heading back east to Denver.

I think traveling by car or train sets its own peculiar cadence, imposing a rhythmic personality which transcends the form. Airline travel can't do this. Except for periods of unwanted turbulence, there is no rolling motion. Flying in the air is just flat. If I can choose, I'll pick a car to get me there: I hope that I might see something of the countryside that's worth remembering for the time and place.

As we headed westwards to drop off Isabelle, we chugged through winding canyons, and I watched a train snaking its way alongside the Green River in the Flaming Gorge. My iPod, playing through the car stereo, filled the space with Enya chanting *Anywhere Is*.

The sound was mesmerizing, rising and falling, rolling along with the train, and I pushed repeat, grasping at words that spoke of new beginnings at the edge of the horizon and separation from what was familiar. I sensed we were losing Isabelle; I sensed that was what she wanted.

It was a lightning-fast trip. After 2 days and 1080 miles logged, we pulled into Walla Walla. And while the town may have been the ambrosial land of sweet onions and wine, we were so drained of energy there seemed no reason to taste it. We limped through a brief tour of Isabelle's college campus and then limped to dinner at a local French bistro.

Even Isabelle looked dazed.

"At first, this trip felt like we were on vacation," she explained. "Except I knew we weren't. We were always transitioning. Then, it began to feel like we were dropping me off at camp."

Dr. K and I sat, sipping Washington State wine, listening to her decompress.

"I don't know why, but somehow I feel like a bird after it hits a window," she announced. "It's a being-in-shock sort of numbness."

The next morning, we left her to find her way. Isabelle went off to be oriented, hurtling head-on into the debate team's early season prep sessions. We said our goodbyes, knowing that although we'd text and talk over the phone, we wouldn't see her until Thanksgiving.

On the way back to Colorado, I decided we were going to take it slower. There had been an exit off Highway I-84 I had noticed as we sped through Oregon on our way westward. I couldn't catch its name as we'd raced past. The signs were just a blur.

There were several bedraggled buildings, a gas station, restaurant and motel, all boarded up. Dr. K reduced our speed and I caught a glimpse of the name on the exit sign, which too had been struck across with large lettering. 'Exit Closed!' it declared.

The hamlet was called Farewell Bend. They were in the process of building a new bridge, and while under construction, all signs of humanity were shuttered.

Farewell? Or fare thee well? Here on this barren stretch of Oregon highway, the name's antique formality was meaningfully anachronistic, harkening back to days when pioneers in covered wagons headed westward on the Oregon Trail. Farewell Bend was the end of the trail, the last stop before travelers left more civilized country for the rugged unknown.

Dropping off a kid at a liberal arts college in Washington State is hardly unexplored territory. But for both parent and child, it's a new world. I like to think that when we drop our kids off at school, it's not goodbye, it's farewell. Do well. Stay well. Be well while we are apart.

THE CURIOUS ATTRACTION OF STRAWBERRY FLUFF

SEPTEMBER 7, 2012

It's a perilous decision to grocery shop when hungry, but even more so in September.

Let's just say there are times when I break the cardinal rules. But I have to admit I'm not quite sure what a cardinal rule is.

I've researched them to figure out if cardinal rules are listed in a big red book of rules — because cardinals are red birds — but even Google wasn't much help. I found several websites listing the seven cardinal rules of life, but none agreed with each other. There were websites devoted to cardinal rules of business, dating, baseball, bookkeeping, and paraphrasing, which makes me suspect cardinal rules can be made up on a whim. Someone declares *these* are the rules for a designated topic, they're stamped with a big red stamp, and it's a done deal. Suddenly, the rules have become cardinal.

The one thing I know for sure is that when I go to the grocery store hungry, there is no question I'm breaking one of those big red rules. And as you'll see, breaking a cardinal rule has the potential for causing a ton of trouble.

What happened wasn't entirely my fault. We're closing in on the end of summer, and I'll be the first to admit I'm sick of tomatoes and zucchini. Both have been prolific this summer.

Most days, lunch consists of leftovers eaten at my desk. Because it's September, those leftovers contain some assortment of zucchini and tomatoes. But on Tuesdays, as a reward for accomplishing the grocery shopping, I buy lunch at the deli. I try to keep it healthy and look for salads dressed with vinegars. But when I stopped at the counter to purchase lunch last week, all I could see were salads and pastas swimming in mayonnaise.

In the back row, shimmering and cloyingly pink, was a confection resembling cotton candy. It was labeled Strawberry Fluff salad. Hungry, and frustrated about the lack of any palatable choice, I asked the deli assistant why in the world they would carry such an item? That's when I learned that Strawberry Fluff is one of the most popular salads in their case. The *salad* is concocted with thawed Cool Whip, cottage cheese, and fruit shrapnel — all encased in red jello. If red jello isn't appealing, there is one made with orange jello with matching fruit. I think that one was called Orange Bluff.

I ended up skulking home with my groceries and ate leftover zucchini-and-tomato salad. I also paged through the dictionary, confirming my belief that *salad* is composed of greens and vegetables and tossed with a savory or piquant dressing.

But first, I let the poor deli manager know exactly how I rated his offerings, breaking another cardinal rule: don't blame the messenger. I knew I had gone too far when I told him the food in his case was contributing to America's obesity problem. Maybe the words just slipped out, I don't know. Or maybe I'd lost it.

"There are lots of things which are worse to eat," my sister Michelle consoled me when I confessed to my guilty tirade. "A macaroni and cheese loaf, for one," she offered, describing an unusual blend of pork, beef, cheese and macaroni noodles pressed into lunch meat. Michelle assured me she knew people who considered it a delicacy.

It's true, everyone is entitled to their own comfort food and traditions. There is no explaining why I like gefilte fish, that traditional Passover food made of a salty colorless clump of matzo meal and white fish. People either love it or hate it. Loaded with the hottest horseradish sauce I can find, I think it's irresistible, but only once a year on the holiday. Avoid it like the plague if you can't find any horseradish sauce.

I also love butter and wouldn't consider cooking with margarine. I hope there aren't food police who would stop me, but I think butter eaters are a protected legal entity. At the Iowa State Fair this summer, the hottest thing going was deep-fried butter on a stick. Supposedly it tastes like a cinnamon roll. As much as I like butter, I'd skip it. But I wouldn't stand in the way of people who think it's divine.

Even so, I couldn't get Strawberry Fluff out of my mind. A week went by and I was back at the grocery store. I'd decided to purchase some pink fluff to see what the attraction was. Humans are attracted to that which we know we shouldn't have.

I told my sister Michelle about the plan. "At least it's pink," she said. "It matches the strawberries. It's how strawberries are supposed to look."

She reminded me about my obsession with food and color. When we were kids, I used to dot packaged French onion dip with green food coloring because I was convinced it was a more appropriate hue.

"Colors elicit certain reactions in people, they have many meanings," Michelle reminded me.

Except they didn't have Strawberry Fluff this week. "We have to rotate the salads," the deli assistant explained.

I went wild. I ordered a container of Pineapple Pistachio Delight, pale green and studded with Lucky Charms — or possibly they were pastel marshmallows but being all mixed together, it was hard to know for sure. I also ordered a container of the Five Cup Salad Dessert — clearly the greatest oxymoron in the world or a food offering which is seriously conflicted as to its identity. That *salad* was an attractive butter yellow, perfectly colored if it had been an Easter dress.

"What are you buying those for?" the youthful checker asked me. After he'd tossed the fifteenth bag of produce down the conveyor belt, his question seemed natural. The kaleidoscopic salads didn't match my profile.

"It's an experiment," I chirped. I was determined to be nicer to store staff than I had been last week.

"You're braver than I am," he said.

Do you want to know the truth? After one bite of each, I tossed the colorful *salads* into the trash and whipped up a plate of zucchini-and-tomatoes.

It's fine with me if others want to indulge in deep fried butter on a stick or an entire carnival of fluffy salads. Each to his own taste. Homogeneity in life leads to dullness and lack of innovation. Right?

Or do you find this all simply fluff and nonsense?

THE TERRIBLE TWOS: WHEN THING ONE AND THING TWO BATTLE

FEBRUARY 22, 2013

The battle between real life and life on paper is a valid excuse for accomplishing nothing.

I was sitting in the row in front of the exit row on a tiny airplane last weekend returning from a college visit to Isabelle, when an unnerving thought hit me.

First, you must know that the specific seat is essential information. It's that seat which cannot, does not, and will not recline.

Caddy-corner from me was a toddler playing a game on an iPad of squash the fruit (best as I could decipher), with the volume turned up full blast.

Sounds of squish-splat-phlatt reverberated across the aisle, bounced on the seat in front of me, and landed in my lap.

In the row behind me was another kid. He was playing *Battleship*, or whatever sort of seafaring vessel makes pinging sonar noises. It could have been submarines or whales, for all I know.

And while I marveled at the state of technology available to amuse youth in-flight, in spite of my (unwilling) upright seat position, all I could muster was relief that we were past this hands-on stage of child-rearing.

I slouched down into the seat and sipped a Heineken and contemplated where things were in my life.

While we do have two college students to visit periodically in far-flung states, I still have one two-year-old in the throes of temper-tantrum stage. My blog, *Feeding the Famished*, turned two on February 12th.

Two-year-olds can be tiresome, at once loving and approachable, then turning brutally independent as they make attempts to break free from their parents, trying to prove their individuality.

A parent may ask herself, "What did I do wrong to create this fearsome behavior?"

The right answer is that a toddler's actions have little to do with direction from a parent.

And while a blog is not flesh and blood, at times, the process of writing seems to be a living creature with its own mind and personality, one with a vision which does not necessarily configure with mine.

How can that be? How can you separate what you write from yourself?

Over the past two years, I've written 162 blog posts, some of which have had greater popularity than others.

I never know which topics will trigger a reaction. As most writers do, I have an array of notes, one-liners, articles, and suggestions from friends, which, one day, will be inserted into *something*. I may not know precisely into which *something* — be it a book or blog post — a tidbit might fit, but I do know it will find its place at some point.

There are a lot of free-floating bits which are wonderfully appropriate, incredibly meaningful, and burgeoning with promise. Every day, more bits are generated and catalogued. As with an angry two-year-old, they will eventually find their way. The developing neuron pathways will connect and peace will reign.

But in the interim, all of these seemingly inert jottings make a lot of noise.

The commotion is in my head, and is compounded by daily visits from a recognizable pair of perennial two-year-olds from childhood literature, Dr. Seuss's Thing One and Thing Two.

Thing One (all the things I would like to write) and Thing Two (all the things in my life to which I've committed) do not always see eye to eye. Much of the time they are at loggerheads, busily asserting that what they need me to accomplish is most important.

Thing One is art, Thing Two is real life. They are inseparably intertwined. One cannot exist without the other.

At times, my mind is like a Rolodex on hyperdrive. I walk through the aisles of the grocery store and a helpful clerk pops out of nowhere, asking if I'm finding what I need today.

My response is usually a blurry, "Um?" because I wasn't listening to him. I was sorting out the voices in my head.

I'm not crazy, at least not certifiably so. There are just a lot of thoughts being processed in there, being assigned to what I envision as a room-sized piece of furniture with many drawers, like the ones they used to have in an old-fashioned general store.

This turmoil isn't unique to me. It's part of the human condition, this tension between our many selves.

At the moment, the days are predictably stuffed full. There are emails from friends to arrange dinners out, committee members reminding me of duties I need to do, and phone calls from delivery trucks and my general contractor, who is making repairs to the mess in our basement after it was flooded with water after a pipe burst.

A text flashes across the screen of my cell phone, a request from my son to remind him what time his flight home is for spring break.

It is followed by another, this time from my daughter, who has butterflies in her stomach. Operating on minimal sleep, she has permanently settled into panic mode, walking across a college campus one thousand miles away from me to take the first of her two midterms. And I'm supposed to fix that with a reassuring text.

Next, Dr. K texts a reminder that he has a meeting tonight, and simultaneously emails an article from *The New York Times* about the status of gender equality since Betty Friedan. Have I had a chance to read it yet, he emails?

I sit down at the kitchen table to read the article, when an accusatory text from my son flashes across my cell phone screen:

Mom! it yells silently, because I have not yet sent his travel itinerary.

And I'm bleary-eyed this morning because, unhappy with this week's blog post, I've been calculating how to restructure it.

Meanwhile, Edgar and Neha, an emotionally needy young couple I've introduced in Chapter Seven of my new novel-in-progress, *Drinking the Knock Water*, woke me at 2 am to tell me their great idea for the direction Edgar's character should take in the next chapter. I told them to shut up and go back to sleep, but by then it was too late. The idea — which was a good one — had now been firmly planted and I couldn't stop mulling it over.

My book characters, much like the real people in my life, contribute regularly to the process. I welcome their intrusions because when at last a thought or concept enters my subconscious, Thing One takes over, and once past the trouncing, independent stage, establishes an unhindered flow of thought.

I begin to relax as I type the words, watching as conversations unfold. The mind takes over, leaving behind dilemmas of whether or not I should broach a subject. The topic plays itself out before me across the computer screen, steered only by the words' caprice.

These are the times I look forward to most, those pleasurable days of productivity, be it on behalf of either Thing One or Thing Two.

These things are our inner imps, striving to be heard, struggling for attention. Much like a two-year-old, this mental activity, directing our days and nights, seeks validation that the actions we take are on the path of progress.

THE MOM WITH KALEIDOSCOPE EYES

MARCH 8, 2013

Being a fly on the wall, college version 1.5

I know at least half of you are going to hate me for what I'm about to say, but it's something I've got to get off my chest. Actually, I would bet upwards of eighty percent of you will disagree with me.

There was this rock group — they don't exist anymore — but during their heyday, you could say this band of musicians achieved a high level of popularity. In fact, this group gave heft to the label 'rock star'.

Before they hit it big, there wasn't much you could associate with the word 'rock', unless you were talking about moving dirt, typically a soil and rock mashup. If you were venerating somebody's achievements, it was also fine to call a person a rock. That meant they were big enough to hold up their end of a building.

But the 'star' part of the phrase 'rock star' makes less sense when you put them together. Sure, people could be called shining stars — that meant they were really good at something or they wore a lot of shiny lip gloss.

Or it could refer to stars in space. About the time these musicians became popular, there was a lot going on up there in outer space. Moon rocks were a subject of much fascination, as in: do moon rocks exist? Which is harder, moon rock or earth rock? Because this is very important to know. We Earth dwellers want to be known as having really hard rocks in the interstellar community.

The crazy thing is, this band of musicians wasn't shiny at all. Shaggy and kind of cute, the 'rock' label was odd, even if compared to moon rocks, which are kind of boring. Back then, no one knew what moon rocks looked like. This bunch of guys became supernovas before anybody had direct evidence. They did it wearing boring black suits, white shirts, and ties, looking as if they were off to a college dance.

Just in case you haven't figured it out, I've never been a fan of The Beatles. The truth is out, and my rationale is complicated. I don't dislike their tunes, which are perfect for dancing.

Where I draw the line on admiration for an art form is: can I understand what the lyrics mean?

I know. Songwriting doesn't require lyrical truths.

Songs are poetry set to music. They are supposed to make you think, summoning from deep within yourself personal experiences that, upon reflection, will help you sort out the mess of your life. Songs are visceral like that. They're no good unless they affect us at gut level.

But The Beatles, those cute, shaggy beatniks from Liverpool, set out to mess with our heads.

They sang about walruses; yellow submarines; poor, misguided Maxwell with his silver hammer who went around banging people on their heads; an octopus who enjoyed gardening; and fields of strawberries. Anyone who knows anything about gardening knows very well that while it would be nice to have eight hands for weed-pulling, strawberries do not grow in fields! They grow in beds, and the stepped ones are the best.

Lucy's kaleidoscopic eyes are particularly confusing. I always thought it was a song about flies.

Because flies — their myriad compound eyes arranged like a layer of tiny bubble wrap over their horned faces — are the luckiest creatures in the world! They can see so much! Each lens, purposefully positioned on a convex surface, provides fascinating input to its owner — the sticky-toed fly — enabling the insect to see quite a lot of stuff.

The input must be dizzying.

As a parent of two out-of-state college students, I identify with the sticky-toed fly.

When we dropped off our son Harrison in Iowa almost four years ago, we parents, along with the other incoming freshmen students, went through orientation alongside our kids. This seems to be a new thing. After my parents dropped me off at college in the Eighties, I didn't allow them to come back to town for months, and then only if they were buying a fancy dinner.

These days, new students are oriented on how to navigate their new collegiate surroundings. At the same time, we parents were oriented away from our kids. 'Go away,' was the college's message. 'Go far away. Do not be a helicopter.' Whup Whup.

That's when I set up a Facebook account.

Facebook, texting, iChat, and mental telepathy would function as my compound sticky-toed fly eyes to help me figure out what my kid was up to.

With two kids away from home and all of us living in three separate time zones, I've found it can work, to a point.

There are all kinds of kids. Some do not want to share what they're up to with their parents on social media.

Then there are mine. They tend to post random and far-flung thoughts on Facebook, anything that dribbles through their minds at any given time of the day.

There have been a few posts which I have questioned vociferously:

Mom: *I think there's something on your Facebook timeline this morning.*

Them: *I didn't do it!*

Mom: *Were you in the room during the happening as described on your Facebook post?*

Them: *What was it that actually happened?*

Next comes that big watershed OMG moment, the one when the hungover, or work-weary, kid — it wears many faces — gasps, and acknowledges.

Them: *I must have left my laptop open during the party/in the lab/when I was in the debate prep room/while I was sleeping/fill in the blank, Mom. Somebody else posted that!*

As the parent living far, far away, in a land which is attempting to be forgotten, there are benefits to taking a sticky-toed fly peek, close up.

We do this about two times a year (per kid) and end up being surprised by what we find. Or rather, amazed by the truth.

When you visit your kid in college, if you really want to find out what their life is like, you want to be a fly on the wall.

That's when you can watch them from a fly's length distance. That's when you see their one-on-one interactions with their peers.

You listen to actual conversations, observing facial expressions as they happen. All those sticky-toed fly compound eyes are active. They note everything, from what the other kids are wearing, to how they greet your children.

You can see how much your kids are studying. It's detectable from the circles under their eyes.

There are all sorts of methods for acquiring knowledge about other people. A fly with its kaleidoscopic eyes gathers a lot of visuals. But how much can you ever know about what's being processed inside someone's head?

The key is access to a continuous stream of information. There are many ways to obtain it, and I'm not sure if any are the best. Keeping the lines of communication open is the key. Without that, there is nothing. And with a little trust, we can work it out.

SOMETIMES THE MOUNTAIN PUSHES BACK

JULY 25, 2013

Cycling is an exhilarating sport. In the thrill of the moment, it's easy to forget how dangerous it is.

For the past three years, pulling our bicycles out of the shed has taken on greater meaning. The action used to have a simple purpose, signifying that spring was approaching and bike season was just a tune-up away.

Where we used to casually cycle a fourteen-mile round-trip to breakfast (because the only reason I exercise is to eat), our mileage has increased. As a result, pedal-pushing hurts a bit more.

It seems we've become more serious about cycling.

In addition to increasing mileage, I find we are testing ourselves against Colorado's many peaks, climbing ever-steeper grades and swooping down majestic mountain curves, leaning into them, allowing the sport and its exhilaration to pull us in.

It's easy to forget how dangerous it is.

There are so many worthwhile rides to support, but we had friends who were keyed in to the Courage Classic. The ride supports the Children's Hospital Colorado Foundation in Denver, which Dr. K and I agreed was a good cause. The mileage was frightening — 157 miles over three days — and so were the names of the peaks to conquer. Day one was Tennessee Pass and Battle Mountain. It finished with Vail Pass, riding up the steeper west side, an elevation gain of 1831 feet in 8.7 miles. Heading eastward towards the Plains, that segment scared me to death.

That first year, all I wanted was to finish those three days without making a fool of myself. And that meant riding the day one passes without collapsing into tears.

After day one, the other two days weren't as frightening.

Mostly, I worried about a nasty section of Vail Pass, a section I happily walked the first year. Any avid mountain cyclist knows where it is: three miles up, after the gate on Old Vail Pass Road, around mile marker 185. Cyclists dream about it, mostly in their nightmares.

Mile marker 185 is when your options are cut off.

There is no sag wagon, no right of first refusal. No return to sender, no way out other than to keep pedaling.

Immediately after crossing beneath Interstate 70, there is a tough pedal up, steeper than the average seven percent grade which Vail boasts. The path borders the highway. As you grind along, four-wheelers in SUVs either cheer you on or comment on your lack of form.

I didn't care that I walked it; many others did too.

Year two riding the Courage Classic was about the same.

Dr. K and I rode a bit faster than the first year, finished the three-day course, and amazingly enough, found that we didn't hurt so much this time.

There are certainly gunners out there, the ones who get up before daylight and subsist on PowerGel diluted with water. They ride for time.

That isn't us.

I suppose you could label our group the sociable 'People from the Plains'.

We ride with friends and it ends up being a mini-party.

You sign up as a team, and the effort is supported by the entire group. That's the mentality of it: we collectively pull for each other to make it up those inclines and get down the steep, winding turns in one piece.

There is well-earned downhill careening. It's expected if you've pedaled up the perimeter of a mountain.

We all remain cautious and respectful of the rest of the group, our fellows.

But for year three, I was bound and determined not to walk up that hill on Vail Pass.

There is no real reason to fear it. It was only an imaginary obstacle to surmount, one segment of an entire ride. But it was a segment that bothered me; its steepness, its gritty noise, edging the barrier of the highway. People comfortable in their cars driving skywards watch you and comment on your struggle.

For year three, the ride added another leg, up and down Fremont Pass, bringing day one's mileage to eighty, rather than the usual fifty-eight.

By the time we hit the feared hill, the ends of our ropes were fraying.

As I began the climb, the ratio of walkers to riders was about equal. I could hear Dr. K pedaling behind me. I knew his breathing pattern by now.

I crested the top and heard a loud crack on the pavement.

Within seconds, there was confusion and shouting among the riders.

"A man is down! A rider fell head first!" the riders yelled to each other.

Dr. K was closest. He had passed the cyclist and asked him how he was doing, but received no response.

Our fellow rider lay face-up, half on alpine grass, half on hot pavement. Dr. K checked for a pulse but couldn't find one. He, several other riders, and a Courage Classic Medic performed CPR for over fifteen minutes until the firetrucks and ambulance arrived, too late, from their uphill trek.

Watching the death of a fellow cyclist on the Vail Pass biking trail brought the extreme nature of the sport into focus.

Day two dawned and we suited up, ate breakfast quietly, and checked the weather. I noticed tension in my chest that morning as I struggled to gain the stable platform of a second wind.

Yesterday had subdued us. No one mentioned the rider's death, but I sensed we all wondered: will this next turn of the pedal bring *my* last breath?

The scene on the edge of the mountain highway replayed in my thoughts for the rest of the weekend, interlaced and threaded together with a greater question: why?

Why did a sixty-one-year-old experienced rider break away from life so quickly?

I crested a little hill bordering Lake Dillon. The path's edges were studded with banks of purple wildflowers, caught in the sun glow of early morning. Around the next curve, idyllic sailboats sat seemingly motionless, frozen for a moment in time as I sped around the corner, and then they — and I — were gone.

There are many reasons to ride a bicycle.

It's a good time for contemplation, of the possibility of God, for the observation of nature.

On the final upwards climb back to Copper Mountain base that day, a rider in front of me extended his arm, the palm of his hand facing towards me. That's the warning to slow down. A mother duck and her ducklings were attempting to cross the bike trail.

Several days later, back home again and reading the newspaper I'd missed over the weekend, I read my horoscope for that dark day on Vail Pass.

It said every cloud has a silver lining. There was nothing wrong with slowing down. It said that if I did, I might avoid a pothole, even though I wouldn't know why, at that particular moment.

PLEASE HOLD WHILE WE COME TO OUR SENSES

AUGUST 28, 2013

No one likes waiting for life to happen.

Life seems to be centered on waiting for the thing we don't have, for an occurrence we wish would happen (right now), or for someone else to take the next step so we can move forward with our plans.

But there is an unnatural discomfort about waiting.

We understand it is part of how transactions with the people around us function. Even so, we rail at invisible nothings when nothing is happening.

We realize there are times when we have no control, when our expectations are not totted up in a gigantic scorebook, one that tracks life's positives and negatives. This fact does not make us happy.

This past summer has been defined by waiting.

Our house is up for sale and we have bought another. We wait to see who will buy ours, longing for that transfer to take place so that we may begin again. We are waiting to play house somewhere else.

Harrison, with a new college degree, waits for graduate school entrance test scores and the opportunity to pursue studies at a European university if he is granted a residence permit in time for matriculation. He hovers over his choices, the potentialities of where life might take him.

And Isabelle: she counts the days until she can go back to school.

It isn't that she hates us. It's that she is a teenager.

All of her friends are there, in the Mecca. They've been there all summer long, free-spirited and independent. Half in jest, she emails me a BuzzFeed link all the way from her bedroom. In it, she shares a list of the sixteen obviously rational reasons why she has been driven to the point of near insanity by living in her parents' house after sampling one year of college in another state one thousand miles away from home.

By the time we are all packed up to take her back to school, I am as ready as she is to hit the road.

It's hot in Colorado and we have just been treated to one of our freakish hailstorms, the kind which consume the sky. They are storms that seemingly come out of nowhere, creating a rolling barrage of destruction across the Plains. These are darkened-cloud days where swirling skies resemble *The Wizard of Oz*. Except it's not amusing or even remotely charming because there are no Munchkins and it is our house which is at risk.

We leave for the drive westward, glancing back at our ravaged house and garden. I don't worry much about the flowers; once trimmed, they will revive. I will talk to them quietly. I hope they will understand that no one controls the skies.

The skylights on our roof are another thing. There are five of them, all shattered by hailstones over one inch in diameter, leaving a five-hole punch in the ceiling. I perform a reverse rain dance daily, futilely negotiating with the cumulus clouds that float blithely above our heads during monsoon season: please don't rain. We're trying to sell the house, and the carpet in the attic playroom is beautiful.

I know this looks like a call against nature, that in our part of the country we want — no, we need — the moisture to water the crops to feed the world.

But it is my attic that will get soaked. We don't venture up there much. It's the perfect spot to store things, the things we don't need right now.

It houses all of my son's belongings from college, all the kids' toys, all that stuff which is waiting to be transported to the next spot, wherever that may be.

So, we leave our home in the hands of the weather forecasters.

Sometimes, it's healthy to run away from home for a little while. When you're waiting for things to happen, at times, it's good to be in the middle of nowhere.

We found ourselves there soon enough.

Our Chevy Suburban, The Great White Buffalo, (now renamed The Great White Golf Ball, a credit to all the hail pocks) surges forward to its new home in Washington State. We're allowing Isabelle a car since she didn't flunk out her freshman year.

Despite The GWB's bulk, it dances a road waltz, following the highway's dips, and swaying in time to Sarah McLachlan. She warbles *Drifting*, a song about running from your past, with loved ones left behind with only a forlorn hope for your return. And I wonder, is this where we are headed with Isabelle?

Lunch is a brief, dusty, stop in Sinclair, Wyoming at a fifteen-table hole-in-the-wall with a cracked and grimy sign outside advertising Pepsi. The name of the soda dwarfs the name of the restaurant. Inside, we order platters of Mexican food, burritos laden with spicy green chile, tinged burnt orange. It warms our tongues and spirits.

After, we fly past the Flaming Gorge exit, and then a billboard advertising the wonders of the Mummies of the World exhibition, all the way on the edge of the continent in Portland, Oregon.

Dr. K wants to know what kind of mummies they have there, and I tell him, "Dead ones."

My mood isn't the sunniest.

In the backseat, Isabelle's conversation flits from one friend's text to the next. For tonight's dinner in Salt Lake City we'll be joined by this college friend, and would it be okay if another one joined us for dinner in Walla Walla tomorrow?

Since the first day of summer break, she's kept a countdown on the mirror in her bathroom, tracking the days until she can go back to school.

I don't mind. Her happy chatter is a far cry from the worried silence of last August as we drove her west for the first year of college.

And then we find ourselves headed home, waiting again, on a small airplane.

Hanging in the sky, all activity is suspended. I feel trapped and gullible as we ride the jet stream of delusion, because I am still nowhere.

The SkyMall catalogue is my friend and I leaf through it, even though I know I should be working on my novel instead of this mindless activity.

The catalogue on the tray table feeds on my weakened emotions at having just dropped off Isabelle, but in spite of them, I begin to giggle uncontrollably.

"Do people really buy this stuff?" I ask Dr. K, pointing to the Inventor's Corner, where you can purchase stick-on collars to 'double the life' of your dress shirt. They're like the license plate renewal stickers I gum onto my car every fall, layer over layer, except that no one is looking at the ring around my license plates.

There is an interesting contraption, the Rollie™ Eggmaster™, which claims it can cook raw eggs into cylinders, which seems odd, since there is no electrical plug, from what I can see in the ad. I could buy a new best friend, a voice-activated R2-D2, which reverts to an 'occasional bad mood mode'.

I've recently dropped off my teenaged daughter at school, so decide to pass on that opportunity.

There is travel gear, hearing boosters, and shoes promising to cure plantar fasciitis, but what takes me off the charts, leaving me helpless with laughter, is the Porch Potty, premium version.

Are there really people who are so gullible that they would consider buying a plastic container topped with 'plush synthetic grass, scented fire hydrant, and outdoor self-drainage' so their dogs can relieve themselves inside the house?

Even if I thought about purchasing the premium version, the one with the embedded sprinklers and 'automated rinse and drain system', the one I can own for only $279.99 (plus a $5 delivery charge), would I be in my right mind?

Probably not, is what I've decided. There is an element of delusion that takes hold when we find ourselves waiting for life to happen.

Back home again, I'm sitting at my desk, writing. Flopsy sits at my elbow, begging for a used Kleenex.

Her breath smells like frog. I know she's been munching on them. It's still summer, and if you were a collie, wouldn't you take advantage of the smorgasbord out in the yard?

She waits patiently, knowing I will relent and scoot a used Kleenex across my desk in her direction.

I think she's deluding herself. Why would a dog want a Kleenex when there are plenty of fresh frogs for the taking?

FINDING THE BUBBLE

SEPTEMBER 13, 2013

Egg metaphors are perfect for describing people. Good eggs, bad eggs: you know what that means. It provides a common ground to explain personality.

Have you ever been stumped when trying to describe a person you know to someone else? You want to explain a situation, based on another's personality, and there you are waving your hands in the air and saying, "Well, you know, he's a lot like Jack. You know my friend Jack, right? The big lacrosse player, the guy with curly red hair with a big gap between his front teeth? The one who —," but all you're getting is a blank look.

This is the germ of frustration, when you find yourself at a loss because there can be no meeting of the minds. That's when it's good to find some common ground and figure out a home base to bring it all into understanding. That's when eggs come in handy.

Everybody knows what an egg is. Eggs are not simply nourishment and little cholesterol hoarders. Inside the circumference of that delicate shell, eggs contain the spectrum of human personality and emotion.

There are good eggs and bad ones. The bad ones are truly rotten. They can smell, and they represent a wide range of nastiness, from people who merely disappoint, all the way down to the very worst of the lot, the pirate bad eggs, the ones who are happy to maraud, pillage, rape, and torture, all in the name of rotten egg-dom.

If my friend Jack happened to be a really bad egg (which he isn't), you would know exactly what I'm talking about.

There are old eggs, the ones past their prime, and if you become embarrassed by something you did, you've got egg on your face. If you want to broach a topic delicately, it's best to walk on eggshells, and no one who wants to get ahead in business puts all their eggs in one basket, unless they want to risk breaking an egg in their pocket. And of course, there are the eggheads, not those who are lacking in hair (as I once thought), but rather those whose pretentious intellectualism puts us off because they prefer to leave the rest of us behind to wallow in the mud of pop culture. Oh, the horror of it all. I guess I'll have to watch *Downton Abbey* all by myself.

Eggs can be very useful organisms, if it weren't for their mystery. Those shells hide a lot of essential information.

Take my son Harrison, for example. He's a fairly typical college graduate. His future is promising, if only he could figure out what he wants to do. Which was why we agreed to his request to visit a friend in Sweden immediately after graduation.

He thought he should apply directly to medical school, but then, possibly not. *"Wouldn't it be great to be a world explorer for a little bit?"*

Two days after he was handed a diploma, off he went. The game plan was that, on his return, he would knuckle down and study for the medical school admission test.

Two weeks later, he was back on United States soil. I hadn't heard from him much, except for a post on Facebook saying that yes, he'd figured out the vending machines at the Copenhagen airport, and was able to buy a train ticket to Lund where he hoped his friend would meet him. Other than one picture of the two of them enjoying coffee and cinnamon rolls in a garden, that was it. He was off the radar.

On his return, he was a whirlwind, brimming with new and wonderful ideas. He would apply to a Swedish university for a master's degree in biochemistry, taking time to enjoy Europe along the way. After having grown up in a little town on the Plains, we thought it was an interesting idea — considering that, when he was nine, all the traffic in Denver freaked him out, and even though he was a good skier, he didn't have a Nordic bone in his body.

Even so, over the summer while waiting to be admitted to the Swedish university, he promised he would study for the med school entrance exam.

Why Sweden? you might be wondering. The answer to that is simple.

1. The Swedes are really nice people (Harrison informed us) and they all speak English;
2. It's cold in Sweden, and Harrison likes to wear sweaters; and
3. Swedish women are beautiful…

Anyway…

As we simmered the egg, there was one unknown, a not insignificant one. To be able to study in the country, a residence permit was required. As an American, this is a difficult concept to wrap your head around. After all, we were paying for the degree and it sounded like a great experience. Harrison is a nice kid, he works hard. Who wouldn't want him in their country?

Not so fast, you might say. Rules are rules, they're in place for a reason and everyone has to abide by them.

The egg timer ticked away quietly, minutes winding down to seconds. At 1:30 in the morning on the day he was scheduled to depart we still didn't have the residence permit.

"Let's put him on the plane," Dr. K suggested. "We're six weeks out from applying for the permit, it's close to being granted, I'm sure. He can explain that to them when he lands. He's a nice American kid and he's got the acceptance letter from the university."

Scenes from the movie *The Terminal* popped into my head. They might deport him. Or he could end up living in the Stockholm airport, just like Viktor Navorski, until the permit is granted. He would miss the window to matriculate into the university and we'd have to mail him care packages of Annie's Homegrown Shells & White Cheddar Macaroni & Cheese, except he might not have boiling water to cook it in.

I frowned at Dr. K. Sometimes, being an egghead isn't all it's cracked up to be.

But there was a stray eggshell in the batter. Harrison had received the results of his medical school entrance exam only hours before. They weren't all that bad. I hesitated. Dare I broach my idea to the nascent world explorer? I might be shot down in mid-flight, scalded in boiling water, or smothered in hollandaise (Mm, not a bad idea).

Call me stupid, or call me intrepid. At 1:30 in the morning, as Harrison sat in the kitchen playing a game on his Nintendo but worrying about life, I decided to tap the shell.

"That score you got today on the exam, that's a game changer, you know?"

I ventured this thought, proposing the idea tentatively. "You don't have to go to Sweden. You could apply to medical school now."

I waited, expecting to be fried, boiled, or scrambled. What did I know about adventuring?

"I don't want to go to Sweden," Harrison said. "What I really want to do is work in a clinic and get hands-on experience. I can do that here. That's better, I'm being productive and I can apply to med school now."

It was nearly two o'clock in the morning. I was getting bleary-eyed and possibly not hearing right. *Really? All summer long, you've been preparing for this Swedish gig! I'm supposed to put you on a plane in eight hours so you can get deported!*

When you simmer an egg, you never know what you're going to get until you crack open the shell. If it's soft-boiled you're after, that elusive three-minute masterpiece, anyone who's tried to figure out perfection knows that this is an impossibility. I've got it down to three minutes, thirty seconds, if I'm reading the bubbles in the pan correctly, *if* the egg was immersed in the water at the precisely precise temperature, if only all eggs were the same size.

As if.

Then there are the hard-boiled ones. You tap on the shell, and it all seems so right. You find the bubble, the sweet spot that, once you get to peeling the shell, it comes off in one connected piece. It's nice when that happens. It was meant to be, except you don't know it until you begin tapping on the flimsy calcium carbonate that encompasses breakfast.

The truth is that you never know what's going on inside a person's head, even inside the heads of people you've hatched. Unless they let you crack the shell.

A FABLE: THE KIDS WHO DESTROYED THE LEGOS

APRIL 26, 2014

While my kids' destructiveness with their playthings used to frustrate me, I now see there are lifelong benefits to building and repurposing Legos.

If you've never stepped on a mislaid Lego brick in your kitchen in the middle of the night, you are just as likely unaware that Legos have a wide color palette. In fact, Lego brick hues are as numerous as those you shuffle through while agonizing over the decision whether to paint your living room Sherwin-Williams Exciting or Outgoing Orange.

My kids' newest Lego set is molded into tiny bricks in muted shades of tan. Each plastic brick has an exacting placement, each is irrevocably important in telling a tale of lost mummies and intrepid adventurers. As with grains of desert sand, each brick in its chosen shade, once combined with its fellow bricks, tells a precise tale.

This newest set of Legos has been strewn in careless swaths of color across the attic playroom's cream Berber carpet.

Similar to Lego's molded precision, on the Sherwin-Williams swatch, SW 6641 (Outgoing) is only three color blocks apart from SW 6647 (Exciting). But if you step back and take it all into serious consideration, I suppose the differences are monumental.

The more interesting question is this: how does Sherwin-Williams distinguish between an orange that is Exciting and one that is Outgoing?

To my critical eye, Exciting is a less dynamic expression of Outgoing. And yet, both are equally satisfactory shades of anemic tangerine. I could slap either on the walls of the room labeled 'forbidden', so called because it houses a mostly unplayed piano and uncomfortable furniture.

The forbidden room has a formal tenseness, one of carefully selected period pieces appropriate for a neo-Georgian house accessorized with breakable antique porcelains and unapproachability. It is for that reason that the wall color must be precisely right.

The forbidden room is in direct contrast with the mess upstairs in the attic.

There, two children reign supreme. They couldn't give a damn that they have full Lego sets from *Star Wars*, with X-wing and Y-wing fighters, an Imperial cruiser, and Queen Amidala's shiny Nubian Royal Starship. There are also sets based on *Pirates of the Caribbean*; *Indiana Jones and the Temple of Doom*; a fire station; the Underwater Explorers; and two castles, one molded in medieval gray, the other in Belville's pastel pink, yellow and blue.

Complemented by winged Lego fairies and a fountain, its spray of water forever immobilized in glittery plastic, the Belville castle is the outrider of puberty yet to come.

To keep everything by the book, the medieval gray castle sports gargoyles and a cannon.

Each set arrives from the manufacturer with the bricks hermetically sealed in plastic bags. They are separated by color, shape, and size. The children eagerly unfold minutely detailed instructions, align each piece according to color, and build their next miniature masterpiece.

They do build each and every one. The pirate ship, the Gungan sub, Harry Potter's beloved Hogwarts School of Witchcraft and Wizardry — all grow, brick by millimetered brick, snapping slowly and surely into sturdy reality.

Here, privileged childhood decked out in 3-D fantasy is played out and admired.

But the admiration stage is brief.

Once built, after hours of painstaking labor and agonizing reference to the instructions, the models are quickly destroyed.

The bricks' next iteration was probably not intended by the Lego creators.

They are torn apart and repurposed. What began as a red fire truck now finds itself the mottled central character in a Barbie movie. Piloted by a tan mummy, it will be attacked by vengeance-driven, screaming Beanie Babies riding X-wing fighters hell bent on a tactical mission.

Beanie Baby command central is an immaculately painted, stuccoed, and shingled Queen Anne dollhouse. It was built years ago with oversight by Dr. K and his minions, the two brats who dominate the attic.

These days, the brats have moved beyond toying with fancy dollhouses for dollhouse purposes. Instead, they alternate turns with the video camera, filming action for a feature movie set to music.

While the brats' destructiveness used to frustrate me, I now see there are lifelong benefits to building and repurposing Legos. The kids are products of the harum-scarum attic playroom, not the untouchable anemically tangerine living room.

That's why it didn't surprise me how Harrison took charge of his post college gap year.

With his sister off to college, we had enjoyed an entire year of empty nesting. And then he was back.

I looked forward to his return with a mixture of anticipation and dread.

We hadn't seen much of Harrison over the last four years. Even during our college visits, he was either running a race or sequestered in a lab, engaged in study. What sort of person was he now?

I soon found out that the kid we visited at school in Iowa was driven to excel in every area of his life. He had become a whirlwind of activity, leaving no corner untouched. In between filling out applications for different grad school pathways, he ran endless miles. He volunteered at a local healthcare facility, and coached distance running and pole vault.

"Running," he explained, "defines me." The pursuit of the sport had taught him discipline, endurance, and how to focus on a long-term goal.

"I am a runner because it pushes me to go past the pain when I don't think I can give any more."

He debated with himself and us: scientific research or medicine? Which track should he pursue?

He sat in the forbidden room for hours at a time playing the neglected piano, revisiting classical pieces he'd learned when he was thirteen. After running through those he learned new ones while listening to them on his iPod, fiddling with the fingering until he got it right.

He complained of a relentless backache but continued to run, until one day he decided he had no choice but to take a break. Competitive running takes a toll, one that is hard to admit when you are only twenty-two.

Because when you are twenty-two, life is an unfolding Lego map of instructions. There are seemingly endless sets yet to be built and admired. But he mourned being temporarily sidelined from running. It had defined who he was, and at twenty-two, tunnel vision doesn't allow for considerations into the future. Without being able to run at that precise juncture in time, what was left?

A friend encouraged him to sign up for an organization called Bike & Build: Pedaling for Affordable Housing. She had made the two-wheeled cross-country trek during two summers, days of boundless energy.

"Biking — that's for old people," Harrison informed us. "You and Dad, that's fine for you, but it's not the same as running. That's just me and my legs, it's all I need to get places."

But it was his gap year and he had little else to do.

Part of the requirement of preparing to ride from Nags Head, NC to San Diego was to raise $4,500, a daunting amount if the limits of your fundraising experience is selling wrapping paper in fifth grade.

Then there was logging 500 miles in the saddle.

Calling it 'conditioning', the Bike & Build folks advised prepping his body for the 3,592-mile cross-country ride.

Harrison dragged his feet. The time spent riding 500 miles before he hopped a plane to North Carolina was offset by fear of capitulating to maturity. With each pedaled mile he was no longer running by himself. Each mile brought him closer to joining the cadence of adulthood.

Not long before he was scheduled to leave he finally began cycling, brick by brick, mile after mile.

As he prepares for this journey, sometimes we pedal together. Now he is the life coach and I am the student.

He studies cycling skills, passing along his knowledge to me. With Harrison acting as teacher and coach, we are both growing.

After college graduation, he returned home, back to his familiar bedroom. He had expected a period of downtime, time spent evaluating where he was, yet planning the next step on his life's path.

He was frustrated; it lacked immediacy. Undefined, he wanted answers now because he knew what he wanted next.

Or so he thought.

In that time vacuum, there was a silence: initially against his will, it temporarily prevented him from moving.

And in that vacuum he discovered that even when you're standing still your mind is in constant motion, working its way forward, moving you to the next level.

If you're building bricks according to the manufacturer's directions, you might never get there. But if you let it, if you look between the spaces in the bricks or build them into new shapes based on a design of your own making — the next step is possible.

IT'S A DOG'S LIFE

MAY 24, 2014

A history of home moving in eleven steps.

Ihave a perennial attraction for strays and the forlorn, those who are lost, those who are lonely.

One example of this personality flaw plays out in the size of our home. With six bedrooms and a pool house, it attracts human strays, particularly our son Harrison's friends.

But when Harrison graduated from college last summer and returned home, he informed us our house was too big. We needed to downsize.

If you consider Kemme family home history, you'll understand we primarily move for dogs or kids. We've moved eleven times over the years. As is typical, we listened to Harrison and put the house on the market. We could find another home to fix up!

Half the moves can be placed in the 'attending school' column. Easy ones all, we'd call Dr. K's brother-in-law Jerry, a genial guy with a karate black belt who loves to pick up couches and heavy boxes. A week or so before moving day, we'd let him know we were transitioning.

"Again?" Jerry always asked.

We could count on him being perplexed. Moving isn't a concept he gets. He and my sister-in-law have lived in the same home for over twenty-eight years. They found that perfect neighborhood: lushly green and secluded, its winding streets lull passersby into peaceful somnolence, tightly interweaving people of all ages so they never want to leave.

Sheepish, we nod at Jerry, afraid to admit how wanderlust is in our blood.

He'd sigh and stacking three boxes one on top of the other, begin the lug-fest.

Those sorts of moves were quick, from one apartment to the next. We'd begin early in the morning and by nightfall, what little furniture we owned was in place, the kitchen unpacked, the freshly painted apartment-white walls adorned with poster prints.

Jerry, Dr. K, and I would stretch out our legs, order pizza, knock back a few beers, and marvel about how easy that had been.

Then we got a dog. This necessitated buying houses. Houses are different from apartments, the biggest difference being that you are allowed to make nail holes in the walls and nobody cares since now the walls belong to you.

We soon realized there were bigger, more expansive possibilities for destruction. The lure of improving a home became an unshakeable obsession.

The first projects were small, but replacing kitchen appliances and grimy linoleum expanded like a math compass. Making a nail hole wasn't nearly as much fun as tearing down the entire wall. While we're at it, let's dig up the backyard, replace the roof, and realign electrical wiring. Paint and carpet? Yeah, we'll get to those, but first we need to move the kitchen sink from point A to point B. Oh, the smell of drywall dust in the air, lung-clogging, eye-watering.

When I tell friends that we like to remodel, that there is something special about revitalizing an old home and in so doing unwrapping its inner beauty from fusty fetters — not to mention orange shag carpet — they look at me like I'm from Mars.

Our latest home purchase has all that and more. It's such a complete overhaul that, unlike our four previous houses, it will be impossible to live in while we're gussying it up.

Some (smart) people opt for a small condo rental or apartment when engaging in massive home improvement projects. But there was no place to rent in town, no landlord who would willingly (unless we paid exorbitant sums of cash) allow us to bring along our four-footed collie children, Flopsy and Mopsy.

I was becoming wild-eyed with worry. Our house was finally under contract but we'd given little thought to the next step: all that *living stuff*.

Over steaks and martinis, we reviewed this dilemma with our friend and contractor, Bud. He suggested that although we could live in the basement while he created hell-on-earth above our heads, we could instead put expansion quarters in the driveway. We could still access the bowels of the house, using its plumbing when nature called, but the future would look brighter without clouds of drywall dust in our eyes.

I wasn't sure what he meant, but even so, as with all starry-eyed home purchasers in the first throes of new home love, it all sounded romantically do-able.

That's when Bud recommended we buy a fifth wheel to preserve our sanity.

"What's a fifth wheel?" I asked him.

Enter Mabel, a 36-foot fifth wheel trailer. She's real purty, that gal. And while typically people buy fifth wheels so they can hook them up to their big-ass trucks and go tootling around the country in bring-your-own-camper-style, Mabel was going to just stay put in our driveway.

Unfortunately, the furry children we decided to live in the trailer for are scared to death of it.

"Those high metal steps — the way it rattles and shakes when we bound from one end to the other. Mom, no," the dogs' worried brown eyes tell me.

To cement our horribleness as collie parents, while we reconstruct the drainage system there is temporarily no yard.

The collies, they do not like it, not one bit. Mopsy leaves me protest poop deposits all over the soon-to-be-torn-out orange, lemon yellow, and lime green carpet, letting me know just what she thinks of the changes in her formerly complacent life.

We do not like the dirt and mud.
We do not like your contractor, Bud.
We do not like the Backhoe, Bobcat, and Monster Truck.
Those metal beasts scare us, we're feeling stuck.
We do not like them here or there.
We do not like them anywhere.
Back, back we're going to our lush green grass.
Remodeling, Mom, is a pain in the ass.
So take them away, away far from here.
Or away we will run, back to the yard we held dear.

Dr. K and I pet, cajole, and calm them, and still our furry children are nervous. We have compounded the original sin of moving from the house they know to one that almost doesn't exist at all.

Moving to a new house is an adventure but it's hard to explain to an animal. I wracked my brain, thinking about what to do to start them on the path towards acceptance of their new surroundings.

I rifled through leftovers in the refrigerator sitting in the garage, a relic from the house's kitchen we had already torn out. Its doors were off-kilter and hard to close, the vegetable drawers were cracked and dirty. But it was useful overflow space, something we needed given Mabel's mini-fridge limitations.

When I found a container of chicken and rice soup, I knew I'd solved the problem. Feed the dogs chicken soup! If it's good for humans in distress, why not animals?

Stacked high above my head in the garage, I shuffled through boxes. I unearthed a martini shaker and made an inconceivable discovery that Mabel's refrigerator makes ice! Boon number two for the collies: they love ice cubes.

This is all good news. I thought you would like to know about it. Come visit. The bar is open.

HUNGRY, BIRD-BRAINED, BATTERED, AND FRIED

JUNE 13, 2014

I can highly recommend running away from home every now and again.

D o you listen when, unasked, people tell you what you ought to be doing or thinking about in your life?

I don't. I doubt you do either.

Most likely, your mind is already made up. You've crossed that line and waded into the deep end. And like me, you probably didn't notice how the middle of the pool was sloping downhill.

Even so, friends try to explain to me just how wrong I am about nearly everything. For example, when we moved from our fourth house to the one we live in now, people gave me their opinions. As they might a wayward child, they began placatingly enough.

"I love your house, Emily, so why are you moving?" they all asked.

But then, after a pleasant enough opening salvo, the conversations veer radically, pushing me into a hermetically sealed, airtight box. It's a stifling place where they can trap me, place a dunce cap on my head, and insistently harangue, "Why would you ever want to sell it? Why would you consider leaving it? Why would you think you could live in a fifth wheel named Mabel in your driveway while you remodel a crumbling house?"

There were enough unrelenting 'whys' in each lecture to confirm what I had already suspected: I was crazy.

But enough of the whys, already. The closing documents have been signed and filed with the county clerk. It's as done a deal as you can get.

What I really need is someone to hold my hand and explain to me why there are birds living in my new garage.

I suppose you need to know that this new garage space doesn't currently function as a place to park cars. The physical aspects of it are beautiful to behold. With berths for three cars and a floor sprinkled with tan-and-pink pebbles neatly encased in clear resin — a near magical process that never ceases to amaze me — I know that someday we will park cars in this awesome garage. Until then, the space exists to tantalize me with its possibilities.

From a vantage point of the two-foot square window next to my side of the bed in Mabel the fifth wheel, I can see the physical demarcation of our new garage. It represents a portal to Fantasy Land. I walk through the garage and into the dilapidated house, imagining how it will soon return to life.

Each morning, I slide up the pleated shade on the camper window and survey my new kingdom from on high. It's not as celestial as it sounds. There are four perforated metal steps to reach the ground. I worry I'll miss one and pitch forward, cracking my skull on the concrete wall two feet outside Mabel's front door.

Assuming this hasn't happened, I enter the garage, greet Flopsy and Mopsy the collies and head inside, dodging large, black birds.

I know that part isn't in most people's plans when they fantasize about remodeling their dream home. But this is real life and there are birds living in my garage instead of parked cars.

Because we have no yard (torn up), and the collies have no grass on which to run and play (soon, says my contractor, soon!), we leave the garage door open for the dogs all day. They need shade. They need their dog beds. They need familiarity.

But the damned birds have discovered the dog food. Darting and swooping in arcs in front of me, the birds are in my space. They are in my portal to fantasy land!

Remodeling is stressful enough. It impacts my writing creativity. And now the birds have doubled down on the stress.

So when Dr. K invited me to accompany him to a medical meeting in Chicago, I jumped at the chance to escape. After a whirlwind of packing and moving, agonizing over whether the house would close and then making minimal headway towards adapting to life in a fifth wheel, I needed a break.

It was a chance to run away from home for a few days! No black birds chasing me out of my garage! No dangerous metal steps to climb up and down all day! Five days in Chicago! What idiot would say no?

This break was going to be all about getting my head back together so I could work.

"You can go to your meeting," I informed Dr. K, "and I'll hang out here in the room and work on my novel. I'll just write. Fifteen hundred words a day, promise!"

Off we flew, me and my grand ideas traveling together in a bundle of wishful delusion.

But once ensconced in the beautiful hotel room, all I could think of were the birds in the garage. All my mind could conjure were images of the damned black birds cackling it up in my new garage, dive bombing for dog food.

Sitting in the hotel room staring at the computer screen, I dawdled and wasted time, pretending I was researching topics. What I really was doing was surfing. Stray words drew my attention like bright, shiny objects, and my mind darted and swooped, picking at tidbits of information. I needed to clear my head of them, flush them away.

There is a winding path that edges the Chicago River, the waters pulsing westward from Lake Michigan in an alarmingly green hue. Even though St. Patrick's Day is months past the river hangs on to remnants of its celebratory dye.

I jog toward the lakefront trail, passing a kiosk advertising urban kayaking. Glancing again at the vegetable-bright river I decide to forego that opportunity.

Jogging makes me hungry, as hungry as the swooping birds in my garage, and equally narrow-minded. The quest to find momentary peace and quiet, a chance to calm my mind from the recent move flutters away, replaced by thoughts of breakfast. All I can think of are eggs: where can I find eggs?

On that first day in Chicago, I walk and walk, discovering a bright, yellow hallway where they offer eggs. They must. They have named the establishment Yolk.

Dr. K and I keep in touch during the day. I suspect he's angling for a word count but there isn't one. I can't tell him I've written nothing, not after my exhortations that with peace, quiet, and an expensive hotel room, I will be able to write rafts of words. But when he texts, not one to lie, I'm at a loss of what to say.

Dr. K: *Whatcha doin?*
Me: *Walking to a brunch place called Yolk.*
You??
Dr. K: *Bet they have eggs. Just finishing up lunch.*
Me: *What gave it away?*

Bastardized versions of pop music bump and grind, bouncing off the room's narrow walls. I'm drowning in a sea of yolky yellow. *This wasn't a good idea*, I think.

The next day, after another long walk I try Eggsperience, hoping exercise will settle my mind and release words trapped in my brain. This restaurant is square, its coloring less garish. I have high hopes for rejuvenation until the odd antics of a couple behind me trap my attention.

The man rises from their table, once, twice, and then once more, each time taking a stroll around the restaurant. I watch him loop the room, returning to report to his girlfriend about the conversations occurring at other tables. He switches places with her three times, whether to better observe other diners or to whisper in her ear, I don't know. The couple pick on their waitress about the bitterness of their coffee and ask her several times why the menu doesn't offer turkey sausage.

Standing in front of me, two waitresses bicker over which of them had swiped the condiment stand off the other's table. It was me, after mine mysteriously disappeared. I'm afraid to tell them, afraid they may kick me out before I can finish my meal. The vibes in this place are odd.

And then the music thumps, the bass booming, and it all fades away. Thoughts tumble out from my fingertips onto my iPhone screen.

I can't hear the screech of human conversation any longer, and the words spill.

THE THINGS THEY AREN'T TELLING US

JUNE 27, 2014

There are times when we find ourselves getting off the information grid, and in those gaps, we leave the world behind.

Our house took a direct hit from lightning last Saturday. Of course, if we're going to be sticklers for accuracy, it wasn't actually a house. Because we are in the middle of a full house remodel and are currently living in Mabel the fifth wheel, a tin can on rubber wheels parked in the driveway, the potential of being struck by lightning has been an ever-present worry.

The incident was an ideal way to jump start the National Weather Service's lightning safety awareness week, 2014. It's uncanny when real life mirrors public service announcements like that.

After sharing the news with friends (both the real-life kind and on Facebook) and doing a bit of research, I learned that the probability of your house being struck by lightning is 1 in 200. That certainly eliminates the rarity factor.

I calmed down after rationalizing that, as long as we're not one of the almost 50 people in the United States who are killed by lightning each year, a lightning strike is a mundane reality.

But there are serious side effects when your 'house', i.e. fifth wheel, is struck by lightning.

That 30,000-amp bolt can fry your internet connection, and with one hefty zap, wipe out all of the seemingly quotidian methods of communication we take for granted.

This isn't simply an inconvenience. I've discovered the loss of easy access to the internet gets expensive. One friend similarly zapped had to buy a new computer. We were luckier. We replaced the fried modem and router, but in the interim, I ended up with eight half gallons of one percent milk in the refrigerator. Without instant computer access, I became untethered. I forgot to do the weekly milk bottle count and never changed the online milk delivery order.

That's small change, not enough milk poured down the drain to cry over.

The true casualty is the loss of independence. It comes with the discovery of how, thanks to the internet, we are inescapably tied to the rest of the world.

That's when you understand how getting zapped by lightning doesn't fall into the same category as the 'Pick up the phone and call your neglected grandma' pigeonhole.

Neglecting to call grandma is a willing suspension of that thing called obligation. We elect to ignore pleas to communicate with our grandmas, most of whom prefer phone calls over Facebook posts.

Not being able to access the web brings one's identity — that very sense of self — into question. Calling grandma is just rehashing what we already know to be true.

The internet is how we share what is happening in our lives. A smidgen of important information is lost when we go off the grid.

To stay in the game, first I tried the tag team method, using my iPhone to create a hotspot. Dr. K, Isabelle, and I quickly burned through our account limits.

I discovered many new tidbits of information I had never before thought essential. You can't be on the internet and have a meaningful conversation on your phone at the same time. When hitching a ride on a hotspot, you make a choice: internet surfing or talking with your inside voice.

I also learned over five days of disconnect that what people post on Facebook, share in an email, or tap into a text isn't the whole story.

And I learned how meaningful conversations carry more weight than people's Facebook posts.

It's all about what people aren't telling you.

This discovery came to light in a Facebook post I read last week — one from a friend who I actually do talk to in person once in a while — because of what he wrote in his post that didn't actually say what happened.

The post went like this:

Friend: *Likes France*

That was it. Of course, friends of friends pumped him for more information (because usually he is much more verbose), and we all subsequently learned that although he did like France, he only liked it to the limited extent that it was fine, except for the minor detail that he had been pickpocketed.

This unpleasant experience colored the entire time in France to such an extent that he wasn't motivated to note that he liked France until such time when he returned home, safe and sound. In other words, France would only be liked after he'd left it.

What he posted on Facebook omitted this entire story.

His rationale was that he didn't want to bore people with negativity. Pressed for more, he told all.

It was received as expected. There was an outpouring of sympathy. There were stories of similar experiences paired with psychological musings on why these things happen.

It took the extra effort of everyone else delving into the underlying facts to get to the point. When you're face-to-face with a friend, you can read meaning plain as the nose on their face. You can decipher it from their tone of voice. A Facebook post is as empty as a crumpled note on paper discarded in a trash can. Anyone can pick it up to read because it's meaningless.

My son Harrison posts similar non-information on Facebook these days.

We deposited Harrison on an airplane to Virginia on Mother's Day, along with a large cardboard box containing his bicycle and a duffle bag weighing thirty-five pounds.

He and a college friend were headed to South Carolina to join Bike & Build for a ride across the United States. All 3,592 miles of it.

They would dip their rear wheels in the Atlantic, and ten weeks later, dip their weary front tires in the Pacific Ocean in San Diego.

En route, communication possibilities were sparse. They were, in a sense, willingly untethered.

It was the kids' last hurrah before heading to school to learn how to be a doctor and a lawyer. And Mom was going to roll with it.

Except. I'm used to talking to Harrison every few days.

Our conversations are usually like this:

Harrison: *I just finished my Biochemistry test. My life sucks.*

Mom: *I'm sure you did fine.*

Harrison: *No. I flunked it.*

Mom: *Just wait and see. Tell me what you think went wrong.*

We discuss his feelings after taking tests. We talk about how well, or poorly, he ran a race. While living with us for his gap year, we talked about everything under the sun, including how the world worked, or didn't.

Now all he posts on Facebook are pictures.

There are pictures of happy, smiling people hoisting fifteen-pound bicycles over their heads. There are pictures of happy, smiling people crossing state lines. There are pictures of Harrison, scantily clad, jumping off bridges into rivers, and pictures of him engaging in various activities that are legally questionable. Like the one where he's inching up a sundial's gnomon, the narrow shaft which casts a shadow on the dial's face, telling time.

I guess that's what people normally do on their birthdays. I'd like to talk with him to get his take on that.

I'm happy he's engaging in a worthwhile activity. Making lifelong friends is possible when you spend loads of time with others, working hard, putting in pedal-effort, helping build affordable homes for those in need. Their days vary, with rides as short as fifty-milers, and often over a hundred. I know they need to blow off steam and relax.

I'd like to know more.

Who are these people he is sharing life with for ten weeks? What are their names, wishes, plans for the future?

And why did he climb a gnomon in the early morning hours on his birthday? I'm thinking it was a rite of passage of sorts, but I'd like confirmation.

Students go off and study abroad for months at a time. Military personnel are stationed far from home, often in foreign countries, away from what is familiar.

In those times when we find ourselves off the information grid, we leave the world behind.

Sometimes we go off the grid because of where life takes us. And then there are the times when we are struck by lightning.

But there are also times when we tussle about whether what we post in social spaces might let on as to who we really are. If what we share might allow others to see the chinks in our armor.

But it is those things we do not choose to share which humanize us.

The task remains with our friends to ask the questions, close the gaps, fill in the blanks and therein make sense of the truth of our friends' lives.

TOURING THE RUINS

JULY 17, 2014

Remodeling syndrome is like hospital syndrome. You get sick, and you're lying there, looking your very worst. That's the time when friends insist they should drop in for a visit.

I was scrolling through my drafts file the other day, hoping to find inspiration for something to write about, when I happened upon the silliest email I'd started.

I can remember when I did it. We were sitting down over pizza and beer a few months ago at a favorite hangout and Dr. K suggested we should decide what, exactly, it was that we were going to remodel in our 'new' house.

The concept of new is relative. One man's new shoes are what the rapper Macklemore croons about finding in thrift shops. While not a thrift bargain, our new house looks like it could have been found amongst a jumble of discarded doorknobs and assorted unmatched keys. To sharpen your focus, it sports carpet remnants circa 1970 in shades of lime green, lemon citrine, and a mottled black and white that looks exactly like TV static.

Sipping our beers, we started making plans. The email began like this:

Subject: Home Remodeling Plans
We will be remodeling the following:
– Complete

And that was all there was, because that was as far as we'd gotten.

"Complete what? Complete everything?" I mused, trying to decipher my intentions from months ago, because we are now months into a remodeling nightmare.

You see, 'complete' is a vague reference to just about anything you could possibly dream up that could be wrong with a new house. And in the manner of all things which slide out of control, any house part that has been touched (delicately or not so) has slipped down the path towards obsolescence.

So let's just say complete is everything. We don't need to be sitting down over pizza and beer, ruining another dinner dredging our brains for what, exactly, we are going to remodel.

It's nice to get that decision off the table.

Once you undertake an operation of this size, you grudgingly realize it's going to take time for a complete re-do of a crumbling house. You're going to have to come up with a spot on which to hang your hat while Bud the Builder is jackhammering away at your front porch.

People find this complete remodel of our home amusing. Part of their mirth stems from our current living conditions.

As you know, that's why we're living in Mabel the fifth wheel, the gal who's purty, but a tad smallish.

Don't get me wrong. I don't mind bunking down in small spaces (all 350 square feet of her) for short spans of time. There are some benefits of living small:

- Mabel has an in-house vacuum (the word 'house' to be used lightly). I can clean the entire floor space in five minutes.
- If you must ask your spouse a question or give him a job to do, there's no need to shout or go running all over the house to find him. He's right there under your nose.
- Corollary to spousal communication: if the blower fan is on — as it always is so we don't suffocate from lack of airflow in our 350-foot space — shouting to be heard over that apparatus is required. No need to mistake shouting for anger. It's simply a fact that you have to raise your voice to be heard over the helicopter blades set on constant whirr.
- It's possible to sit at the dining room table, reach into the kitchen to pour another glass of wine, and open the front door to let your daughter inside because her hands are too full of dishes she's just washed in the (real) house's bar sink — the only one not yet torn out that a dirty pot can fit beneath — all without getting up from the chair.

- While you're at it, you can also look out several windows and admire the scenery of:
  - (a) a small tree harboring an empty robin's nest with view of grassless backyard piled with dirt mounds and discarded house parts; or
  - (b) a whitewashed wall of concrete blocks

As you can see, living in a fifth wheel while doing a complete gut of a house is very exciting.

That's why I don't understand how there is so much interest from friends who want to be part of our adventure.

Routinely asking "how we're handling it all", they'll pat our heads and remind us "time flies when you're being creative" or some other worthless platitude. They also ask if they might stop by for a peek at what we're up to, or as one friend framed it, could they swing over for a tour of the ruins?

At first, I thought she was being facetious, but when another friend suggested that our house project looked as disastrous as their flood-ravaged mountain cabin they'd been doggedly repairing, I realized everyone was just stating the truth.

The other part of the puzzle is why our children would want to have anything to do with the project.

You'd think that Isabelle and Harrison would consider this an optimal moment to avoid their crazy parents. According to friend and hiking fanatic Gil, we have dreamt up "the most creative and mean-spirited way to get rid of adult children" he had ever heard of. He seemed envious.

Except, it isn't working.

Isabelle has cheerily taken up residence in a pumpkin-orange, shag-carpeted upstairs bedroom that last felt the cool of air-conditioning some thirty years ago, if ever. The HVAC guy mournfully informed us that the house was never correctly designed for upper-level A/C, so we shouldn't get our hopes up.

And when Harrison perambulates through town next week on his way from here-to-there, he's requested bunking rights on the pullout couch in the fifth wheel. It's a new experience, one he wouldn't dream of passing up.

The kids don't care if there is no yard to romp in. They don't mind that there is the daily possibility of being cut off from the world — ever since the trash men mistook our mailbox for junk. Who wouldn't think so? The box sat in the driveway because there was no other place to put it. Just last week, the trash guys threw it away, mail and all.

The kids also don't mind the dust and dirt, or that if you want to find something essential, it becomes a game of Clue:

Mom: *I need to find the crock pot. Which box did you pack it in?*

Isabelle: *That would be in the box with all the appliances. The one marked, 'Things Mom Will Ask for But Doesn't Actually Use — And Will Be Mad About Not Having If She Can't Find It.'*

Mom: *Oh, right. So it's with Colonel Mustard in the library with the wrench.*

Isabelle: *Yeah, Mom. Something like that.*

Oh, the things we do for family togetherness. Or something like that.

THE POLITICALLY CORRECT HOME REMODEL

SEPTEMBER 26, 2014

As everyone knows, a home reflects its owner. So if you're remodeling, you have to be careful about what sort of political statement people might think you're making.

Taking on a home remodeling project is daunting. Project size doesn't matter. The minute you tear a hole into a wall of your house — on purpose — a sort of queasy recklessness settles in.

Part of what I do to help me with a home project is look at pictures. I look at a lot of pictures. Pictures on Pinterest, pictures in magazines, pictures in books and I take snapshots of homes I find attractive wherever I happen upon them around the world.

"Maybe I'll put a stone wraparound porch on the front of our house," I mused to Dr. K while visiting New York's lower Hudson Valley. There's massive gray stone wrapped around everything in that part of the world.

His response was, "Oh God. Here we go."

That, or stony silence.

But as the principal design decision-maker, I waffle and quail, constantly reassessing the task and asking whether the choices I've made for the look of my house are the right ones.

That's because everyone knows that a home ultimately reflects its owner. I'm not talking about superficial details: the dirty dishes in the sink, unmade beds, towels dropped in damp curves on the bathroom floor. These sorts of extrinsic details either tell people you're a slob at heart or you're too busy to play catch up. What I'm talking about goes much deeper than cleanliness. We're talking inner psyche, here.

For example: what does the color yellow really tell the world about who you are?

With our most recent remodel — which involves tearing out just about everything inside and outside of the house — I've even resorted to reading articles only remotely touching on the topic of home fashion. In that, you might say this genre of research has gone too far. Fear of choosing the wrong color for my kitchen cabinets has pushed me over the edge into the X Games of home remodeling research.

I learned from one article that colors, patterns, and what sort of kitchen hood I selected to catch and channel cooking fumes defined who I was. The colors and textures of my kitchen could determine the persona I presented to the rest of the world.

This particular *New York Times* article dissected the home design psychologies of seven 2016 Republican presidential hopefuls. From it, I learned that if I choose pale yellow kitchen cabinets (which I have done), I ought to be rethinking that selection lest it make me look like a lily-livered coward — or a presidential wannabe. It all hinged on if I chose the right yellow. Choose the wrong yellow and you might as well kiss away the Oval Office.

The biggest takeaway was that what we make of our home shows our taste, or lack of it. It also shows our mettle.

Why else would a company that manufactures wood range hoods to fasten over your stove advertise that their products are 'for discriminating homeowners'.

"What does that mean?" I asked Dr. K.

He said it possibly had something to do with hiring both male and female carpenters, but he wasn't sure.

I looked up 'discriminating' in the dictionary and discovered it could mean 'distinguishing', in a sense that if I picked a hood that was green rather than butter yellow (to match my kitchen cabinets) it would be obvious: my goal was to stand out and not try to fit in. Butter yellow was the safer choice. Butter yellow demonstrated how I am a team player who wants to get along, that I accept other's opinions. Further reading informed me that 'discriminating' could mean I was capable of being 'discerning' about my design choices. This included being careful and fastidious.

All this meant I had to go with the butter yellow hood, right? Carefully fastidious and blending in. She's as smooth as butter, the most integrative ingredient in the fridge.

As I flipped through the hood designer's catalog, hoping for further direction, I learned how a range hood could provide 'elegance' and 'style', and that my 'taste and personality could be perfectly reflected' should I select the company's B-series wooden range hood. There was a photo of a hood in a nondescript color, not really white, not really tan, somewhere safely in between. Beige? Let's go with beige and play it safe.

Shuddering as if awakening from a nightmare, I suddenly realized that, much as I might want to, I couldn't choose the butter yellow (milquetoast!) or eye-watering green hood!

Did I want the world to know I would melt with the first withering look of disdain? Did I want to shout to the world that I didn't blend well with others?

I step away from the glossy brochure, step away from the house remodel, and take a jog around the nearby park. Even as we edge the first week of autumn, the grass is still lushly green and the flower beds, meticulously planted by our city, bloom persistently, sensing in the night's chill that their days are numbered, that winter is coming, but they bloom anyway.

Back now at the house, I look at the empty space above the empty space, at the studs on the wall where someday soon will hang a hood, one that graces my new stainless range. The hood is yet to be built. The range sits in a large crate in California, waiting for a word from the builder that it can be shipped here to me in Colorado.

I can see the range even now in its ghostly silence; provider of sustenance, archetypal hearth of the home.

My skeletal kitchen consists of bare two-by-fours leaking tree sap and glue. Ancient bits of insulation installed during the house's birth over forty years ago cling stubbornly to the bones. The raw wood whispers to me, *There are no limitations to what your imagination can conjure. The only limits to creativity are what you choose to allow others to impose upon your mind. Dress us as you like. Adorn us as you will.*

I venture onto eBay to see what sort of vintage house parts I might happen upon. There I find them: a pair of griffin corbels salvaged from an English village church. Glowing walnut wood enhances the winged beasts' ancient snarls. Orange would make a nice counterbalance, I think.

The interpretations of others will certainly come. And I don't necessarily have to listen.

PAYING FOR OUR PESKY INNER HERO

DECEMBER 12, 2014

The inherent beauty of writing fiction is you can interweave real life impressions and experiences with the vapors of your mind. But sometimes, I'm telling a story that actually happened.

Mostly, I tell the truth. But my friends are sure I'm gearing up to spin a story.

I think the problem lies in the fact that, as a fiction writer, friends who read my posts on Facebook question whether something I post is, shall we say — slightly over the top?

That's the inherent beauty of writing fiction: you can be a dreamer, interweaving real life impressions and experiences with the vapors of the mind. As those vapors drift into the atmosphere, I catch them while sitting at my computer, fingers on the keyboard releasing my thoughts. From that confined inter-cranial darkness, subconscious remembrances decades old are retrieved, feeding my imagination, building new worlds, and creating stories.

Scientific studies have unearthed the scintillating fact that the human brain's storage capacity is about 25 cubic feet, the size of a luxury refrigerator, or 2,500 USB drives. Depending on how stuffed your fridge is, that could be a lot of thoughts chilling in there.

But what I post on Facebook is real life, not a story-in-the-making. Or is it?

For example, a recent post raised questions about a true-to-life experience:

Life Lesson #523: Although it's enticing to venture out on balcony of half-completed house remodel to check on progress, if the temporary door handle only works from the inside, it's probably not the best idea.

Corollary: It's a long drop from the roof.

I posted this on the Tuesday before Thanksgiving. Since then, everywhere around town people have asked me about how I became stranded on the balcony. They want direct, let-me-look-you-in-the-eyes confirmation of the story.

Or maybe it's that a story is better in the telling.

Because, yes, I did venture out onto one of the balconies of our remodel-in-progress, and when I did, the new French door unaccountably swung shut behind me with a near silent click. I say 'near silent' because I heard that click from where I stood at the railing on the second floor of our home where I was enjoying the early morning's pale light.

The sun had silvered the yard below, and on the newly installed — and frozen — sod I had looked forward to for months, ice crystals glittered. I wasn't worrying about what the ice might do to the new grass. I was simply enjoying that moment of cold stillness before life erupted around me again. You know, taking a break from it all to appreciate the transitory nature of an experience before it slipped past into the void of time and memories lost.

Except I had heard that ominous click.

My immediate thought was a panicky *Oh crap*, which is the same thought you would have had if you were up on a balcony when the temperature was fifteen degrees outside.

With that click, the pesky, archetypal superhero — the one we all have inside of us — awoke. Superhero Emily insisted it wouldn't be all that difficult to hang onto the rain gutters and drop down onto the ground.

After a shivery twenty minutes or so spent evaluating my options of (a) waiting around until a construction worker showed up to unlock the door and let me back inside; or (b) find the lowest spot on the roof to jump down, I did the most stupid thing possible. I skittered across the ice-slicked roof shingles to the front balcony, and seeing no one there to help me, jumped.

It was more drop than jump, to be completely honest. Leveraging onto the freezing roof gutters, I wondered if the patio furniture below would support my weight. Wearing only pink, cowgirl-embellished pajamas and a fluffy, white robe, it seemed the smartest thing to do at that moment, and more so since I hadn't bothered to stuff my cell phone in the pocket of that fluffy, white robe.

But the real truth is that when you're freezing in fifteen degrees, your brain doesn't function all that clearly. All I knew was I wanted to get down off the roof.

The problem is, when you're stuck in a position like this — pink cowgirl pjs and all — you don't think very much. They do it all the time in the movies! Why couldn't I jump off the roof like all the other superheroes?

Fiction is built around real-life situations. For the heroic in us all, storytelling ramps up the excitement factor, imbuing us little humans with courage to run farther and longer than we ever thought possible. In that, stories are life waiting to be told.

As it turned out, I was fortunate. I paid for my adventure with a few bruises and aching muscles, whether from the cold or from the exertion, it's hard to say. Nothing too terrible happened.

But, as in true superhero form, I did learn a lesson: always take the temporary door handle with you if you decide to venture out on to the balcony of an unfinished house.

LETTING TRADITIONS EVOLVE

JANUARY 1, 2015

Surviving the holiday season is possible if you and your family practice some escapism during the holidays, and let your family traditions evolve and grow.

I'm whistling a happy tune today. We have survived another holiday season, with all of its inherent expectations for cheer and traditions of family togetherness. Even though we've only just slid under the rope into the year 2015, I'm not ready to put all my shiny-and-hopeful resolutions into effect. I'm not even ready to tell you what they are. Instead, I'm in a reflective sort of mood. I feel like evaluating what we did over the last two weeks of 2014, because it gave me a whale of an idea.

The whale part is important for you to remember — that, and the theory of evolution.

My musings date back to early December, after a friend's comment that Christmas wasn't Christmas when you have teenaged (and older) grandchildren. I understood what she was talking about. Once kids get past age twelve or so, the holiday tinsel isn't quite as sparkly. It might have something to do with a loss of holiday mystique (no Santa spoilers coming, so stop worrying), or it might be that the kids are cresting adulthood. Schoolwork is more demanding and so are their friends. Today's multi-media messaging options have raised expectations that they be part of the larger world, even if that world is circumscribed by the narrow confines of their cell phone screens.

But those expectations create pressures with which we are fully familiar in the adult world. Particularly, teens are subject to FOMO, or 'fear of missing out', an anxiety generated from their tether to social media. The holiday season alters our everyday life: there are more activities, more people to visit. But we can't leave the real world for weeks at a time, nor is it healthy (or even realistic) to enmesh oneself in holiday fun 24/7.

That's why Dr. K and I have always believed practicing escapism during the winter holidays is a good idea.

When Harrison and Isabelle were little (ages eight and five respectively) we began a tradition of heading to the big city (Denver) for a cultural extravaganza. Children of that age have limited attention spans and an appreciation of glitz, so culture was limited to whatever blockbuster musical theater matinee was showing at the Denver Center for Performing Arts. Afterwards, we had an early dinner and headed back home to the relative quiet of country living. Three hours of joyful singing and dancing in candy-coated Technicolor, followed by the promise of french fries with dinner if they stayed in their seats at the auditorium. It guaranteed sleeping children for the hour-long drive back home.

Fast-forward fifteen years: escaping from set holiday traditions has evolved. The Denver cultural extravaganza (and beer fest) now takes up three days and has developed greater meaning. It actually involves educational activities. There is a lot less glitter. And yes, there is some beer-drinking.

Over three days spent in the big city last week, there were meanderings around two different museums: the Denver Art Museum and the Denver Museum of Nature & Science.

After I responded to Harrison's burning question — "What are our plans?" — his reaction was, "You must think we're nerds, Mom."

I hesitated, unsure of what the proper (non-inflammatory) response should be, and said nothing. And then Harrison told me, "I like being a nerd."

So off we went to the museums in search of something new to learn. We garnered information about chemical compounds in rocks, and marveled at how the colors in minerals weren't the shades of green-brown-blue you'd think might be unearthed from deep inside a dark cave. Magenta! Eye-watering chartreuse! Regal purple! There were colors and shapes that could win a competition for best floral arrangement. We saw a 3-D printout of an Egyptian mummy's skull, and I learned how much Harrison and Dr. K hated exhibits about the history of jewelry. But the biggest eyeopener of all was the evolution of whales in the exhibit Whales: Giants of the Deep.

None of us had ever questioned that whales were mammals; that's what scientists said, and we followed their lead. It never occurred to us to consider that evolution played a pivotal role in how that fact came to be. Early on — like 50 million years early on, in the Eocene period — whales were pretty much large rats, looking remarkably like our runt-of-the-litter collie, Mopsy, long nose and all. Environmental changes aided development from water-wading land animals who had a taste for fish into the fascinating whales of today. Interestingly, the whale's closest living relative, based on a comparison of ankle bones, is the hippo.

The exhibit made me think about the benefits of evolution in all its forms.

We knew we had created good family time when there was a segmented chunk devoted to just the four of us, exploring something new, and not all that far away from home. It is a manageable mini-break from the holidays and the rest of the world. The cultural extravaganza is something everyone looks forward to for a variety of reasons. One thing greatly anticipated is time spent in Denver hotels. It's not a necessity — we only live an hour from the city and drive there all the time — and yet, it gives the extravaganza its specialness. A true mini-vacation, it sets that time apart, time that has evolved from a somewhat frenzied afternoon into three whole days.

The winter holidays are not the same as when our kids were small, but there still is the marvel. There is wonder at learning the unexpected. There is curiosity nurtured by imagination and a perpetual pursuit of knowledge and education. There is the fact that, as adults, it's entertaining to sit around a table at dinner and talk with our kids. We don't chase them around a restaurant anymore. While there is beer chilling in their hotel bathroom's sink, there is no more experimentation with the condiments in restaurant water glasses. This year other members of the family joined in, and we spent time with friends, adding layers of variety.

The cultural extravaganza is without doubt a family tradition, one I hope will continue to evolve. I hope it will develop new aspects, each of us adding ideas to burnish those days, if not with the gaudy sparkle of tinsel, then with the glow of candlelight reflected in a polished mirror.

ENCHANTED BY MUD SEASON

MAY 15, 2015

Sometimes, you are given a gift without even knowing you wanted one.

It was early April when Dr. K sent me the email — half apologetic, a bit sheepish — that he had forgotten to cancel a week of vacation after we'd nixed the plans months ago and decided not to go away. He was apologetic because he knew I was swamped with projects and would not be happy to travel — anywhere — at least not in the next three weeks. But maybe we could take off for a few nights, take a road trip to New Mexico, the Land of Enchantment, he suggested.

I told Dr. K no thank you. I do not want to visit The Land of Enchantment in mud season.

Looking at his email, I screamed, I ranted, I gnashed my teeth at the computer screen in my best *Where the Wild Things Are* way that I can gnash teeth. *Didn't he know just how damned busy I was?*

The beginning of May in Santa Fe is mud season: that chilly part of the year when, at a high desert altitude of 7,000 feet, even in that charming city's temperate climate there is some snow melt. It muddies feet and moods. Mud season, or shoulder season, whichever you call it, is that time of year when there isn't all that much for a tourist to get excited about other than hunkering down in front of a kiva in a toasty bar, downing margaritas, wishing for sunshine to dry out hiking and biking trails. The ski area is closed and all the dirt gets ground into the grout between the red clay tiles that pave the city's shops and restaurants.

It's called shoulder season for a reason. It's the season when the rest of the world shrugs its collective shoulders at mountain towns bereft of snow, towns waiting for trees to bud out for summer hikers,

111

world class opera-lovers, and fall leaf-peepers later on. It's time to go to the Bahamas.

Even so, he talked me into going. The second week of May found us on the road. Projects had been tucked in to slumber on their own, to be poked by a stray email to get them back under the quilts. The laundry had been completed twice in one week so we could make our escape. April's and some of May's social obligations had been attended to, and as we headed southwest, armed with reservations for hotel and restaurants, my breath slowed. I began to look outside the car windows, seeing the scenery for its purple mountain majesty.

Because it was mud season, I'd only packed boots: cowboy, to handle mud's grittiness; hiking boots, in the hopes we could hike; and bike boots. The road bikes, stuffed in between suitcases, boosted my wan hope that we might find dry roads.

Santa Fe is an old city. Founded in 1610, it is the oldest capital in the United States. Nestling against the Sangre de Cristo mountain range, the area has known peoples since 900 AD. Age brings wisdom, and with wisdom comes serenity.

For Santa Fe, serenity has been earned over centuries of bloodshed from revolts by the Native American peoples, the Pueblos, and from wars with Mexico and the Republic of Texas. It has endured bloodless heartache, too — Santa Fe saw a Japanese internment camp during WWII, and has felt growing pains as it searched to find its place in the sun, insistently defining itself as a center of arts, culture, and quirkiness.

The plan that first day was a fifty-three-mile ride, over rollers and down valleys.

"Everything around here is flat, you can see for miles," Dr. K encouraged me, playing tour director. "Slight elevation gain, maybe 1200 feet total. We should be able to do this in three, maybe four hours. We can be back for a late lunch."

I nodded in agreement, added a request for a nap, and clipped into my pedals. Off we went into an exhilarating breeze, past charming adobe buildings, weaving through narrow streets, onto a railway bike path, until we came to a grinding halt. We were on the outskirts of town, scouting for the radial street that would lead to the ring road to make a grand loop. We straddled our bikes at the intersection, coaxing Miss Google to tell us exactly how lost we were. The wind buffeted our front wheels in gusts.

That's when we met Steve, a cyclist as equally lost as we, a three-year transplant from Los Angeles.

"What's not to like about the openness here?" he replied, when we asked him why he'd moved away from palm trees and beaches. "All this space."

He was training for the next weekend's century ride, part of which would cover the road we navigated together. He was fine getting from point A to B, but we all agreed point C was troublesome, so we searched for it together.

Steve stayed with us until he was certain we knew where we were going, then jetted off. I was already getting tired of pedaling the ups-and-downs of rolling hillsides. Steve had to be at least ten years younger than we were, and while he courteously waited for the strangers he'd encountered by the side of the road to catch up, it was time to wave him on his way.

Everywhere around us was dry. Dry as mud dries. Junipers and dusty sagebrush dotted the rolling landscape for endless miles, where arroyos, cracked lips gaping, were punctured by yellow road signs warning of imminent rushing waters. Turn around, don't go further, don't drown (you idiot), the signs cautioned.

It is a land where darting mountain blue birds break off from the impossibly blue sky. Living creature or winged mirage, they teased and confused.

We paused in Galisteo (population 265 and declining) next to the Iglesia Nuestra Señora de Los Remedios. Her serene ochre adobe structure ruminated, sitting patiently since 1884, waiting for worshippers to intermittently breathe life. We wondered where in Galisteo we might find water, and straddling our bikes again, continued to ponder that question.

Up and up we continued, back towards Santa Fe, back to civilization, nourishment, and that nap. Where were the easy rollers, the lovely valleys? Where might a tired biker find an energy bar?

Stopping for breath on the side of the road, a biker whirred past. "You okay?" he asked. Fellow bikers always do that, it's part of the club rules. "You want an energy gel?" he asked.

I told him no, I just need to breathe for a bit. I was smarter than that. Didn't your mother ever tell you not to accept candy from a stranger? Even if he was wearing a Steamboat, Colorado jersey.

I sipped my soon-to-be-gone camelback of water. Colorado resident or no, it made sense to be cautious.

We cranked into Eldorado, ten miles from Santa Fe, still ten miles from our hotel. An inaptly named hamlet, I didn't seek gold. It was after two and all I wanted was a sandwich, a beer, and a taxi back to town. I love to bike, but enough was enough, I told Dr. K the tour director. Elevation and wind had tuckered me out.

That was when the Steamboat-jersey-clad Santa Fean sauntered up. Ordering lunch at the deli counter, he had heard my whining, evidently. Major Bob, a retired field artillery parachuter and comptroller for the United States Army, rescued me for the price of a ham sandwich. He scooped up our bicycles into an enormous Dodge Ram truck and took us back to our hotel. We didn't have to buy him the sandwich; he'd already offered to take us.

"You should have taken up my offer for a gel block back there," he chided.

Over lunch in the deli where he'd parked his truck, he shared his fascinating life story. It was worth giving up the rest of our ride to hear it. And on the way back to Santa Fe, I asked him, "So, what is it exactly that you do?" He was a bit intimidating, being an army major and all. He'd briefed Colin Powell in his past life.

"My Mom asked me the same thing once," he chuckled. "I told her I blow things up and yell at people."

"What do you enjoy more?"

He glanced at me across the expanse of truck, and we both knew the answer. It's always more fun to blow things up, but should you actually admit to it?

Day three. I'm beginning to relax; I don't count the miles anymore. Charlie Miner dips a nub of glass into silver nitrate to underlay a tumbler. We're there in his studio, Tesuque Glass Works, to buy a piece of art, a double helix of fish, frozen forever in green glass of Charlie's design. We drove there after discovering his workshop (thanks to Steve, the LA transplant) on yet another grueling bike ride. Charlie invited us to watch him blow glass.

"It's a twelve-minute tumbler," he says perfunctorily.

I climb onto a soda shop stool overlooking the kiln area, while Dr. K ambles around the gallery. Charlie overlays coloring on a deep cobalt base. "It's like cake decorating," he quips over his shoulder.

I learn later that this is standard glass artist patter. It's cake decorating with a 1,950-degree oven.

Communicating to workshop assistants with nonverbal cues whenever he needs equipment, I watch Charlie's silent dance between glowing kiln and bench where he alternately twirls a glob of molten glass, or puffs into a metal pipe to expand the glass ever so slightly. The material oscillates between roughness and a smooth patina of beauty, silky as carved stone, fragile as only glass can be. Temporary as only glass can be.

He walks us through the steps — how he created our sculpture of fish, carving them from wax while watching *Oprah* last winter, the weeks-long process of the lost wax method as plaster is replaced with ground glass, creating a one-of-a-kind sculpture.

"I didn't invent this," he laughs. "The art has been practiced since the Romans." Charlie looks around his studio. "You're looking at a winter's worth of work right now in this studio."

Noticing the full shelves, I had already sensed that. In a few weeks the season will start, the time when Santa Feans will make it or break it for the year. That's when the personalities will tense.

But during shoulder season, I saw the real people of Santa Fe. Lively, warm, engaging, and uninhibited, they shared ideas and experiences, brimming with helpfulness.

I want to return next year. I want to go back to that time of in-between. The time when people are waiting for the next step. The time when they're waiting for the world to warm up.

THE SECRET TO HERDING CATS

OCTOBER 9, 2015

Sometimes when you ride, you start out aimless, without a purpose. You might find one in the silence that exists between you, the road, and your bicycle.

I have a friend named Gil whose primary goal in life, now that he has reached retirement age, is to improve me.

At fifty-three, I can walk, text, and not trip over the curb — all at the same time — and yet, he feels I've got a ways to go.

So far, he has improved me (with Dr. K's encouragement and participation) enough to complete the following feats:

- To bike up (and down) Trail Ridge Road in Rocky Mountain National Park, (where we reached an elevation of 12,135 feet but I forgot how to breathe);
- To ride east over Vail Pass just for fun ("Just pedal and smile," Gil instructed, "because then it looks like you're having fun.");
- To complete Ute Mountain (a mini-climb of only 2,000 feet).

And yet, because Gil is a cheerleader at heart, he believes he is not yet finished with me.

I'm not the only one Gil likes to improve. He has many friends he entices to join him for these workshops. Like bees to honey, Gil methodically implants a project into the darkest reaches of a person's psyche. Once embedded, this nugget festers until the recipient is certain life will never be worth living, that they will be labeled a failure until this challenge is met, dammit.

For the most recent, a doozie spread out over four days, he attracted friends from places as far-flung as Maryland and South Carolina. This time, the implanted nugget was to ride a near-100 mile stretch down Highway 1 in California.

Please note: simply because you point the front tire of your bicycle down geographically on a map does not mean that you have an easy coast downhill. Maps lie like that. In fact, the 'workshop' would entail climbing 7,052 vertical feet.

To be fair, Gil pointed out there would also be 8,006 feet of downhill riding, meaning more down than up.

His commentary on this point was worrisome.

"Going up is just like going down but it takes longer so while going up, you are going slower and have lots of time to look around at the beautiful countryside."

His boundless enthusiasm didn't match mine, particularly when I recalled my trembling hands after a coast downhill on Trail Ridge, a coast nearly as brutal as the upward grind.

There were nine of us at a jovial dinner at a fish house on Monterrey's Cannery Row the night before we set out. We were doctors, nurses, and artists of varying mediums. We were all cats, each one independent and opinionated as hell.

I wondered how this trip might play out, but came to learn my friend Gil knows the secret to herding cats.

It all comes down to this.

Cats are self-reliant creatures. Other than the desire that you feed them, they show little interest in domestication. Outwardly, a cat might appear loving and will seek you out for what seems to be petting and purring sessions. This show of affection is only to ensure that food regularly appears in its bowl.

This is because cats excel at manipulation.

You cat lovers out there are in heavy denial, insisting *your* pet is in fact a member of your family and would be heartbroken without you.

Sure, pro-cat websites promote positive cat attributes: they can be affectionate, playful, quiet, companionable, and smart. But cats can also be stubborn, hissy, arrogant, aggressive, and high maintenance.

From the cats I've met, any whimsical insistence on cat loyalty is simply misplaced hope. All the cats I have tried to introduce into our home wore a collar marked, 'Does Not Play Well with Others', the others being two large collies who assert dominance over our house and couches.

Even so, I believed Gil knew what he was doing with his plan to herd eight cats down the Pacific Coast Highway.

First, it's difficult to get lost.

To your left is mountain, to your right is ocean. We were to embark at Carmel and happily coast into Cambria four days later. Three days of riding, one day of play.

A friend in the computer programming industry once told me it's easy to herd cats. All you have to do is show them a shiny object. Cats are inquisitive and naturally predatory. They love to pounce on laser beams and will chase a shiny light for hours.

The Pacific Ocean, with bright sunlight glinting on its mirrored surface, is the quintessential cat attractor in its ability to lure us cats off the edge of a cliff, searching for an elusive and chimeric brightness.

But as one of the cats to be herded, it was that whole ocean thing which worried me most.

A friend who had just returned from a driving trip along the scenic, coastal road — upon discovering what we were to embark upon — cautioned that the road had no shoulders.

I sort of remembered a statement of that sort. It had been buried in one of the seventy-five emails Gil had sent to the group, one of the seventy-five emails no one had read thoroughly, we all admitted later.

After that boisterous meet-and-greet welcome dinner on Cannery Row, I spent two hours panic-scrolling through websites on my iPhone.

I digested cautionary tales of Boy Scouts who'd nearly plummeted into the sea because their front tire had struck a pinecone. I read warnings about the millions of insane convertible drivers carelessly zigging and zagging across both narrow lanes on pleasure quests, while a warm, Pacific wind tousled the long hair of companions nestled at their sides.

Romance seemed to trump caution on the twisty, tortuous road leading from Carmel to Cambria. Woe betide the cynical cyclist who dared pedal its path.

I fell into a fitful sleep, and dreamt about plunging into the cold and heartless Pacific after an unfortunate bike bobble. And that was after bouncing off jagged rocks and being attacked by the Elephant Seals who dwell near Cambria.

What had we signed up for?

We had a late start on day one. Much time was spent getting nine cats suited up and bikes in order. At last, off we set on a winding road, wending past majestic gated entrances leading to mansions perched on the edge of a liquid world.

We climbed up and over the hallowed Bixby Bridge, a true test of lungs and legs, and suddenly understood that even cycling at sea level wasn't going to be easy.

An hour or so into the journey, I rechristened Highway 1 'Mustang Road' in recognition of the convertibles roaring along it.

As we ground along, I muddled over the art of enticing cats to climb up these steep hills while risking being run over by a speeding red Ferrari barreling toward you in your lane around a blind curve. How do you convince eight other cats this will be fun?

I inhaled deeply. Wild fennel and mustard scented the road, overpowering the stench of sticky tar in spots where construction rigs parked, the graders and bulldozers clinging to the last inch of chip seal as they resurfaced the road.

Farther down the highway in Big Sur, ocean breezes gave way to dark primordial forests, the redwoods sky-scraping, and my neck ached from gazing upwards, impossibly searching for their tops.

Then on to Lucia and its scrappy row of cottages chained together to keep them from going over the edge in a brisk wind.

On and up, past Ragged Point, and then downhill to the Elephant Seal Rookery, where chunky bodies lazed in the sun and young males rousted about in the waves, learning to become champions.

It was all there on Highway 1, all of life offered for the viewing.

There was time on the bike to think, to consider, for quantifying what was important in our lives at that moment.

And I realized that we cats pedaled up a hill and came down a mountain. I suppose we did it because we could, because it was there.

THE THANKSGIVING THAT TIME FORGOT

NOVEMBER 27, 2015

Thanksgiving is a time to pause, a time for contemplation and reflection. It can take place anywhere you happen to find yourself on the planet on that day.

Thanksgiving is the time of year when Americans should never contemplate running away from home, even if only temporarily. Inspired by the good intention of repairing a shredded nation, President Abraham Lincoln decreed a national Thanksgiving holiday in November 1863 after a Union victory at the Battle of Gettysburg. It was dedicated to concepts of family and country.

Based on this dictum, it obviously follows that if a person is fortunate enough to stay close to home and family to celebrate Thanksgiving, by all means do it. Why take a vacation that week? Travel expenses escalate during the winter holidays.

The already slow lines at security crawl to a halt, immobilizing people like lava at Pompeii. Flights are delayed midair, circling and circling like a hawk eyeing its prey — and because it's winter, the weather is precarious.

Why expose your family to hassle? The holidays are supposed to be fun!

That was always my impression of Thanksgiving, my favorite celebration.

My rationale is that I am a first generation American.

My dad was born in Germany. My mom was born in Italy — thanks to a friend of my grandfather's who advised my German

121

grandparents to emigrate quickly out of Germany to avoid Hitler's *Anschluss.* Through my parents' stories, I have learned a love of country.

I am an American and nothing else. I owe allegiance to none other because the United States took in my family. My safe haven is here.

I also like Thanksgiving because the holiday is nondenominational, belonging to no religion or race. And although Lincoln's intention, following George Washington's lead, was to thank God for blessing our country with fortune, the holiday, more than others this time of year, relates more to pride of country, giving thanks for what we have built together.

It's the Fourth of July without fireworks, without summer's sizzling temperatures. Thanksgiving is the more subtly patriotic holiday, but it still recognizes the undeniable benefits of liberty, freedom of thought, and other democratic tenets.

Given all this, as you might expect, all hell broke loose in the summer of 2001 when I announced to both sides of the family that because our children had a week off at Thanksgiving, we were going to take advantage of it and travel to England.

Maybe they were upset because it appeared we were being unpatriotic. Possibly it could have been that we were not going to roast the turkeys that year for the family dinner.

Or it could have been the reality that the kids had reached an age where they might appreciate a trip across the water. As an attorney and English history major, I wanted to show my kids the stuff that had shaped me. The stuff I thought was important.

I booked our flight to London at the end of August. Two weeks later, 9/11 happened.

The planes crashing into the Twin Towers, the Pentagon, and a field in Pennsylvania changed all American's lives. And in that hour of terror, we Americans, who were usually so sheltered, discovered helplessness. And I, English history lover, lawyer, Jewish American Princess, had to decide if I felt safe enough to travel — with children — to England in a world that had turned itself upside down.

I cancelled our travel plans weekly and then, berating my insecurity, rescheduled them.

My nuclear family placed bets as to whether we would actually embark on the trip. My extended family hoped we wouldn't, that we'd be home to roast the traditional turkeys.

British Airways hated me. But Americans were immured in fear. No one wanted to travel anywhere so it was easy to cancel and reschedule. Talking to a British Airways agent became a near daily activity.

And my extended family continued to deride me. I was committing the unthinkable: skipping Thanksgiving.

After the final rescheduling, off we went.

I looked over my shoulder as we boarded the plane in Denver. There were no obvious deterrents: no Saudis toting bombs, no one chanting how much they hated Americans.

We boarded the Boeing 777, seats extending to infinity. Our fellow travelers seemed tense but pleased. We were off on travels, some seeking definition of existence on Earth, others chained to work schedules, some with plans indeterminate.

After dinner and mini bottles of airplane wine I began to relax. The crew dimmed the cabin lights but there remained pinpoints of light, for those who spurned sleep, for those who could not.

Across the darkened aisle I spotted a young man, immaculately shaven, impeccably dressed. I had admired his beautiful cognac-colored loafers when I'd encountered him in the aisle. He sat under a spotlight reading the Koran.

I nudged Dr. K and whispered my fears, "We are certain to be blown up."

He shrugged his shoulders. "Goodnight, Emily," he said, and stuffed his head further down into the thin pillow.

I tried to keep an eye on the man across the aisle, struggling to stay awake, but wine and a sleeping pill knocked me out, a chemical combo stronger than my will.

Tense seconds droned into insensible hours and then the Boeing's lights flickered back on. We landed safely at Heathrow soon after, and my neighbor across the aisle glanced at me and smiled. The Koran lay open on his lap; his smile spoke of relief no less than mine.

All week long, Londoners welcomed us, patting us on our hands, offering hugs, providing reassurance to their shaken confederates, the weary ducks from across the pond.

It Starts with a Fish

The United States was at war with Afghanistan, trouble was brewing about Iraq, and yet there were people of all nationalities, cultures, and races who recognized us as Americans and wanted to let us know they stood with us. They told us: we understand what it feels like to be threatened in one's own homeland.

There were armed police everywhere, draped in orange riot gear instead of the expected Bobby blue, more police than I'd ever seen in London, but once the rawness of it wore off it became part of the cityscape.

And Thanksgiving itself? We hadn't expected to find turkey dinners offered anywhere, and yet they were nearly standard fare — with all the trimmings, so the signs read — on that particular Thursday, November 2001.

We ended up at an Italian restaurant near the hotel, indulging a hankering for the comfort of spaghetti and meatballs.

For us, it was the best safe haven.

NURSE RATCHED'S THEORY ABOUT MEN

JANUARY 8, 2016

The post-op differences between men and women have nothing to do with pain levels, and everything to do with the fact that men don't read their horoscopes.

Every few years here on the home front, I am graced with the title 'Nurse Ratched' by Dr. K, recalling the misanthropic nurse antagonist in the novel and film, *One Flew Over the Cuckoo's Nest*. The number of times I have been rechristened with this title are five: once for each of his surgeries during the course of our (to date) thirty-two years of marriage.

His penchant for renaming me comes with a French door-sized refrigerator box containing all of his pre- and post-op paraphernalia. Last time I took inventory, the box included three velcro-strapped boot casts, five slings, four pairs of crutches (varying heights and materials, all guaranteed uncomfortable), numerous inflatable accessories for your choice of limb (arms and legs only, so don't let your imagination run wild), and several braces (knees and ankles predominate). There should be something for a pain in the ass, but that malady is only in my mind's eye.

There is also a bag full of hastily re-rolled Ace bandages bulging like bloated pigs. Every single one has lost those pronged, metal pins to hold them together. Whoever designed those pins must have been a sadist. The pin's functionality tends less to hold the wrap together tightly, and more to unmercifully poke already-tender skin. All too soon, the quick-to-become inelastic bandage slithers to the floor, a flesh-colored lasagne noodle lying in wait to trip up the newly hobbled.

But the reason I am designated 'Nurse Ratched' by my mostly loving spouse is because I read the newspaper horoscopes and he doesn't.

Dr. K's preparations for surgery reflect his view of how life should proceed, in an unerring straight line.

His most recent surgical adventure involved a little 'dental work', according to one of his surgeon friends. Unlike Twitter's gross-out contests splashed across the internet in brightly Instagrammed and bloody details — it was recently trending a live craniotomy — I won't bore you with the number of metal screws inserted this week into Dr. K's left foot (four), how many bones they had to slice, crack, or smash to accomplish this miraculous recreation of a workable foot and ankle (at least three, from what I can read on the X-rays Dr. K proudly showed me), and where they got the new ligament from.

As I said. Unless you're into zombie movies, there are some things you don't need to know.

When my sister offered to just run over his foot with her car, he declined, although he noted that her method would be cheaper.

Staidly moving forward step by step, Dr. K evaluated what he wouldn't be able to accomplish during eight weeks of non-weight bearing. To get a running start, he tested smoke alarms, changed filters on the heater, and took his rolling scooter on test runs around the house to see how it navigated tight corners. He also reminded me on numerous occasions that he wouldn't be able to take out the trash. His thinking was scientifically plotted and linear.

I have a more global way of thinking. Each morning, I check the seven horoscopes of those near and dear to me and consider whether I should warn them about the pitfalls and perils of their day, or keep my mouth shut. I don't think ahead as to what might happen to Dr. K during the next eight weeks of post-op because I'd have to multiply that by seven people. That's a lot of projected possibilities to keep track of over coffee each morning.

This is Dr. K's sixth surgery. I'm familiar with the post-anesthesia nausea, the pain control, the limited ambulation that so frustrates him, and the fact that he is housebound with me and not at work. Things will happen when they happen, and then I'll deal with it.

His life view comes with blinders that he straps on when he walks through the door from work. While in action, he concentrates on the rest of the world, but at home and wounded, the camera turns on himself.

I, on the other hand, have so much else to keep an eye on. There is always someone to get ruffled over. I'm in a perpetual state of ruffledom over something new that might be predicted to affect one of the seven horoscopes I must watch over.

My horoscope yesterday said it all so succinctly: "Amaze everyone as you juggle balls while riding a unicycle."

I am not making that up.

Perhaps that explains why, the night before his surgery, I had mushroom-clouded dreams of trekking through knee-deep snow for six hours to collect him from the hospital, all the while dropping house-plan-sized rolls of papers I repeatedly stuffed under my armpits to keep from becoming wet. The papers were all very important documents — or at least so my dream told me — that he had to sign to be released from the hospital.

Of course, none of this was real, other than the fact that he'd left the pre-op paperwork on the kitchen table when we'd left home. The admissions staff didn't really need it; everything is computerized these days.

Several hours after I dropped him off, the charge nurse called me to say the operation had been completed and I should come to the hospital to collect him.

My dream told me that if I dropped all the rolls of paper in the snow, he'd never survive the surgery. Even though his surgeon had called to tell me that all had gone well, I wasn't sure. I'd dropped all the paper.

As I walked into the surgical wing, he waved cheerily to me from across the ward. The operation hadn't bothered him; it was the fact of being tied down for eight weeks that did. Like I said, he's a methodological, straight-line thinker. He looks ahead at the long haul. I'm a whirling dervish with fireworks shooting off in intervals in various directions, their trajectory unplottable until after the spectacle has been set off.

I set up rules for healing that are emotional and need-based; he looks to see how fast he can plow through them. Because I must take care of the most basic needs, he is hobbled. That's why I get called Nurse Ratched.

But I prefer to think it's because I read the daily horoscopes, and he doesn't.

LOOK MA! I'M ADULTING!

3/11/2016

Adulting: when you inexplicably find yourself in the slightly uncomfortable situation of gravitating to grown-up, real life actions.

Would I get into heaps of trouble with the Apple thought police if I publicly admitted I do not like Siri? Or if I told you I not only disabled the app on my cell phone, but deleted the microphone button from my iPhone keyboard? I do not want to hear that voice, even by accident. That voice takes away my hard-earned status as an adult.

When someone asks for help solving a problem, it is one sign that the person is taking steps toward adulting.

It's a step in the right direction that Apple gives users the option to allow Siri into their lives at all. As did C3PO in *Star Wars* irritate all the other droids with his know-it-all-ism, Siri the she-C3PO similarly tries to read thoughts, all the while subtly smirking behind her façade that she — knows — best — . And so, it irks me.

It's better to let people try on their own and possibly fail. So what? You got lost and you had to drive around the block one more time looking for the address? It's okay. It'll connect one more neuron to another in your brain. You can explain your lateness by telling the people who were wondering where you were that you were conducting mind-broadening exercises.

Case in point: my sister and I were reminiscing at our monthly breakfast when she mentioned how, when she wrote letters home from college, Mom mailed them back to her, edited for spelling and grammar.

I was surprised at this. My sister is a skillful writer with a good vocabulary. It seemed unreasonable that, should a kid make the effort to write home, that would have been good enough. I was mostly irritated with Mom — she clearly didn't understand that the criticism could chill communication. Maybe she thought she was contributing to her daughter's educational process.

Except, in my experience, the action didn't ring true. Mom has always struck me as one of those people who doesn't tell you what to do. Not that she wouldn't like to. It's more that she wants to see where you might take your own actions, should you decide to stray down that path she knows is incorrect.

For that reason, correcting grammar unasked is out of character.

I've edited my kids' work plenty, but they have to ask me to do it. Like my mom, I've tried to see where things might go, letting my kids make choices. They do fail at times, and in that moment of failure they might bemoan the path they took.

Lately, I'm seeing glimmers that they are learning to adult.

What, you didn't realize 'adulting' is a verb? That's okay. Neither does my spellchecker.

A recent addition to the life lexicon, adulting is what you are doing when you inexplicably find yourself in the slightly uncomfortable situation of gravitating to grown-up, real-life actions.

For example, my daughter Isabelle burst into the house the other day, reciting a lengthy list of to-dos. They included a synopsis of ideas for the syllabus for the class she is going to teach for her honors thesis, the urgent need to restock kitty litter, and the concern that she would be late for an appointment to get the taillight repaired on her car.

"I don't have time today to get juiced or to go thrifting — I really wanted to — but it just isn't going to happen," she informed me. "I'm adulting."

I listened in amazed silence and bit my tongue.

Then there is our son, Harrison, who recently married Alex. He's in his second year of medical school and she has a busy graphic design job in the city. They spent one night honeymooning, but the top thing on their minds the morning after the wedding was how to get renter's insurance.

I get questions on more mundane topics, too. Last week, he called me from the grocery store, out of breath.

"You know that salmon you used to make when we were little?" he asked. "It had two different sauces, but I don't know what kind. So, could I have the recipe?"

When I googled 'adulting', I found a lot of banter deriding the word. It's a method of self-derogation — a put-down in front of your peers. Maybe that's true, but when I've heard the phrase spoken, I can detect a layer of self-satisfied pride. That when a person says they are adulting, they are calling attention to the activity while making a statement: they are ready to move on to the next level in life.

That's a tough thing to do, admitting to your peers that life as you know it isn't enough.

Maybe it's because this generation wants some adulation, an acknowledgment that it didn't take prompting from their parents to take steps towards grown-up-dom on their own.

This current generation seems to take on responsibility, as if, world-weary, they understand the gild is off the lily.

When I consider my children, I see them as more worldly than I was at the ages of twenty-one and twenty-four. They read more about and are plugged in to current events. When I was their age, my nose was in a book. I don't think it helped me grow. While bookish, they take a hard glance away from it every so often. In the long run, this generation will succeed and be happier with the things they have and what they can make happen on an individual basis.

Both Harrison and my new daughter-in-law Alex are into climbing, something you do in a gym, with mats and graspable hand grips and lots of people around to keep an eye on you in case you miss a hold. On a scale of 1 to 10, it rates a 5 on the Mom panic scale, compared to the 11 rating when Harrison was a pole vaulter in college.

I was texting with him the other day, and he casually mentioned that he was going climbing outside. It's spring break and he needs a rest from studying for boards. I agreed it was perfectly acceptable, but what I really wanted to say was, "No! Don't do it. Big, scary rocks! There aren't any mats!"

We didn't talk about it further and I held my breath. I received this text a few days later.

Harrison: *I'm alive! Super fun day!*

Mom: *You know, you are one hell of a nice person.*

Harrison: [shows photo of sheer rock face] *Good thing or a bad thing?*

Mom: *Good thing because you texted to tell me you're alive. Possibly bad thing to send me a picture of what you just did. Ugh! Were you clipped in? On? Whatever?*

Harrison: *Yeah! I was totally clipped in :P plus I did it with a guy who has been climbing FOREVER!*

See what I mean? I think he's zeroing in on that adulting stuff.

STEP BY STEP WISDOM

MAY 13, 2016

Life is more than taking steps forward. Learning happens at all levels, past and future. Step by step, wisdom comes if we stop once in a while to evaluate.

A clutch of tulips pushed up from the parched, rocky soil in our backyard the other day. I marveled at their bravado and wondered what biomechanics were involved for those hardy green stalks to tunnel their way up and out of the dark.

I know — you see it in time-lapse at the science museum — but when it happens in real life, it's sort of cool.

I doubted the plants had enough water to open into flowers — and then several days ago, they blossomed, bright red and cheery. Where had they been hiding over the last three seasons?

This is the third spring in our house. Year one saw scorched earth gardening tactics — no tilling, no pruning, no weeding — while we razed the grounds, tearing through concrete, brick, and vegetation in an attempt to revitalize the property. It rained a lot that summer and mud dominated.

Year two the embattled vegetation was hesitant; some grass and a new patio, with that newborn bareness mothers attempt to dress up with bonnets and frills. The baby can't talk and communication is mostly unformed. But the nascent yard begins to grow and develop into something recognizable, with bits of tender green.

That's why I was surprised to see the red tulips in year three. Step by step, centimeters each day, they must have fought their way up from the depths back into daylight. Somewhere in their cellular makeup they felt their moment in the sun would come, and that taking it slowly, step by step, was worth it.

I know. Plants can't feel like we do. But there must be some impetus to make it happen. Is it only that the harassment had stopped?

My son Harrison is studying for his end-of-year final exams, wrapping up his second year of medical school. He stands on the brink of life actually happening, that breathless moment when one moves from living out of a book and into the real world. There will be more exams, plenty of them, but most of his learning from now on will come from life experience as he develops his professional skills.

He texted me the other day. It was a snapshot of his desk, study guide open and heavily annotated, and in the background was what looked like a screen shot of the Titanic. When I asked him what he was doing, this was what he texted:

Harrison: *I've got this YouTube of the Titanic sinking playing in the background while I study. Figured you'd probably enjoy it too…*

Mom: *It's mesmerizingly horrible! Good study timer, though. When the ship sinks you get a study break.*

Harrison: *I like how it resembles the tone of studying for these exams… I'm currently reviewing everything I've learned all year.*

Mom: *Chug chug chug. But steer clear of icebergs.*

It was oddly ironic, studying for the future while listening to the swishing sound of water as it flooded, washed over, and eventually sunk the unsinkable Titanic. In the background, the ship's great engines groan quietly, ominously, and after the encounter with the infamous iceberg, with warning bells ringing, the ship's crew calling out commands, there is an eerie, hollow echo portending doom.

The YouTube video runs for 2 hours, 40 minutes, a real time presentation of the great ship as it sank to the Atlantic Ocean floor.

There was something in that horribly hollow echo of the sinking Titanic that made me think of step counters.

FitBit, Jawbone Up, Nike FuelBand — those are a few of the gadgets we use to count the steps we take every day, putting one foot in front of the other, validating our existence. Chug chug chug. I've had friends get upset when, after an active work day, they discover they've only taken 2,000 steps. If you don't get in the required 10,000 steps daily, you've failed.

It doesn't matter that pedometers are inaccurate. Ask a physician. He'll tell you it's much better to discuss ways to handle your high blood pressure than to cheer you on about the number of steps you took last week.

There's also more to life than simply taking steps. We all want to get ahead and keep moving forward, but if we don't evaluate the depths of information, if all we are doing is skimming the surface, if all we care about are the false achievements, how do we know that arriving at our destination was worth it? What along the journey did we collect and learn? Did we walk across the surface but forget to account for what was lost? What about the information we might have pulled from every cubic inch of the matter we waded through?

I'm not even sure where *there* is, but we all get *there* eventually.

It might be a better trip if we learned something from the individual moments.

CHASING FRANCE'S PAST TO DEFINE OUR FUTURE

SEPTEMBER 9, 2016

When you're biking up a hillside in France, there's a lot of time to think about how the United States has shared France's revolutions, philosophy, and history.

The other day I received an email from a longtime friend — someone I've partied with, worked with on non-profit events to raise funds in our community, someone I've philosophized about the world with — and I read it, thinking it was going to be one of those jokes, the funny ones, the kind people send each other to lighten the day. Instead, it was astoundingly disturbing.

The email suggested that, since it was clear that conservatives and liberals do not get along, we should give up the ghost of trying to agree and get divorced. It advocated dividing up the United States, creating lines of 'us' and 'them'. In essence, it advocated civil war.

I think the email had a greater effect than intended because we had just returned from vacationing in France.

The choice of France was twofold: friends had invited us to join them for a VBT bike-and-barge trip on tributary rivers on the outskirts of Paris. And three years ago, a long-lost relative who lived in Switzerland had contacted me. We'd been exchanging emails of a quasi-pen pal sort ever since and had wanted to meet. After our families had left Germany — more than seventy-five years ago making a forced emigration to Brazil, Switzerland, and the United States — it looked like the planets were in alignment to make reconnection happen.

But France today? No longer the province of rose-colored glasses, but instead the scene of terrorist attacks. It was the gruesomeness of Charlie Hebdo, rampant antisemitism, intolerance and tension, and blood-washed depictions of la Tour Eiffel shared on Facebook. It wasn't the gilded Champs-Élysées and champagne; it was grittier, with senseless killings at popular cafes. The world grieved alongside Paris for its losses, but no one wanted to visit it.

I've never been an advocate for adventurous living, but I figured — we're going to be on a canal boat on little rivers out in the countryside riding bicycles! How dangerous is that?

So we went to Paris. To bicycle, to hang out with friends, both old and new, to see beautiful French scenery and architecture, and enjoy one of the world's most enduring cuisines.

Of course, I was worried about spending time in France.

Paris was hot when we arrived, a more intense heat than normal for August, and even more deserted than expected for the month when much of Europe goes on holiday. Paris was a tomb, an effigy of itself. The sidewalks rang with our footsteps, the stone buildings echoed our voices when we spoke to each other on the street. It was more than the heat. The empty streets were ominous.

And then there was the unknown of what we were getting ourselves into: the barge itself. Holding twenty passengers and six crew, including our two VBT trip leaders, the cabins were compact, with nooks and crannies cannily crafted to hide away belongings. Two narrow bunks per cabin, several doors, cabinets and a whole lot of luggage made living in it for a week a Rubik's Cube of contortions for every movement you made.

Whenever you're on an excursion — a new experience — at first, there's often an element of insecurity.

The first night on the barge, I couldn't sleep. So I counted sheep.

Except (in my dreams) I told myself that sheep can't swim, so when they jump over the barge, they're going to land in the water. Sheep landing in water are really noisy. There's a splash with each one, a lot of baa-ing, and each time, it wakes you up with sweaty palms, except I was freezing because the air conditioning in our little cabin was cranked up on high.

And then everyone else on the barge began shouting, "Sheep overboard!"

We all got up and pulled the sheep out of the River Seine and now bedraggled, they settled down on the bow of the barge. Everything smelled like wet wool. I went back to sleep.

Day two: after the night's excitement (and no sleep, after saving all those sheep), I was sick. Being sick while riding a bicycle is tons of fun. It's just what you want to do on vacation, and you especially look forward to getting to know your fellow shipmates in between running for the bathroom. I'm not sure what happened to the sheep, but we dined on beautifully prepared chicken, fish, and beef that week on the barge.

By **Day three**, we all were biologically synchronized, communicating unintentionally with that all-too-human flushing in the middle of the night. "You sleeping much?" we'd commiserate. "Nope, me neither."

On **Day four,** everyone was showing pictures of children, grandkids and dogs all around, to the crew, to the guides, to us silly fools on bicycles tootling all over France. We were sweating in the heat together, pulling for each other to ride up to the top of that hill together — because somehow, the mild French countryside had developed quite a lot of hills — and we were sharing beers together at the end of the day on the bow of the barge. If you substitute French wine for grape Kool-Aid, it was like being at camp. I loved it.

Our two guides wore T-shirts emblazoned with the VBT mantra, 'Shake hands with the world'. And much more interesting than the workings of our mutually human digestive systems were the reactions of the people we met in the quaint little towns we biked through each day.

All over the Île-de-France, from Paris to Corbeil-Essonnes to Melun, Fontainebleau to Dormelles, Sens and the fairy-tale village of Villeneuve-sur-Yonne, the French welcomed us, thanking us for visiting. "You're brave for coming," they would say. "But thank you, so very much."

We toured Fontainebleau, the bejeweled chateau of royalty for 800 years, until the French Revolution in 1789. We saw the exaggerated way royalty lived at the expense of their subjects, until the subjects rebelled, until one of their own, Napoleon Bonaparte, soon slept in the bedrooms of kings, replacing a monarch with an emperor, equally bejeweled.

I recalled my French and American history — our shared revolutions, our shared philosophers, generals and social historians. The names Voltaire, Montesquieu, Lafayette and de Tocqueville flitted through my mind as I remembered their writings. You think about a lot of things while pedaling up a hillside in France.

And we sat in darkness with the others on the pavement in the plaza in front of the ancient cathedral of Sens, the stones still sun-warmed from an immensely hot day. Weary from cycling and the heat, we waited for the light show — *Lumiére des Sens* — to project on the stained glass and stone façade of the cathedral.

It was crowded in the plaza, and a graceful, older woman in a white linen dress, her husband and two grandchildren in tow, sank down on the stones next to me. After a week on a barge, I was feeling pretty grimy, and words of dismay escaped, that she would elect to sit on the ground in a white dress.

"It will wash," she told me in French, and we struck up a conversation, me telling her about our cycling trip, she telling me that they had recently moved from Paris to Sens, where it felt safer.

I looked at her, and the barriers fell away. It may have been the anticipation of the light show on the cathedral, the story of which I was familiar. It may have been the heat, or the relief that our trip was coming safely to an end.

"I've always felt comfortable in Europe," I explained. "My family was from here. Je suis Juif," I told her. I am Jewish, or at least that is my heritage.

She studied my face. "Moi aussi." Me too.

And then the light show began, a history of the cathedral from its beginnings over 800 years ago. We stood and watched, as stones were raised, the cathedral built and then it fell, as colors kaleidoscoped in swirls of florals and tapestries, the patterns Gothic, Medieval, Islamic — the East and West merged into one beautiful telling of its story. We stood there together in the darkness, celebrating France, the old and the new.

And then we returned home, to the *Etats Unis*, to the United States. And I sit at my computer, reading the newspaper, reading about the unprecedented political fractiousness, and I wonder.

THE REMOTE-CONTROL GENE

OCTOBER 7, 2016

Remote controls are frustrating because they are a surrogate for ourselves, a tangible example of the many things in life over which we have no control.

Dr. K's sister and brother-in-law were in town recently, and they stopped by the house. The last time they'd seen it was mid-remodel when the house was gutted, taken down to studs and dangling electrical wires. At the time, we were tucked into Mabel, a 350-square-foot fifth wheel that was parked in the driveway. The months in Mabel were a manner of living that has raised eyebrows and evoked chuckles from whomever hears about them.

While touring the refurbished house with my sib-in-laws, I showed them a room, walls painted wrinkled elephant gray, containing only a couch. At least, that's how I view this space with three walls and an oversized frame of stretched, white canvas. While it appears to be a blank space perfect for painting on, Dr. K calls it the 'theater room'.

This space hides a projector that no one can reach, and there is a well-curated collection of keyboards, remote controls, and other plastic gadgets with inexplicable buttons, toggles, and dials that have some connection to the white canvas. There are no instructions.

The collection is loved by my spouse. Me, not so much.

"So, can you turn on the TV, Emily?" my sister-in-law asked.

Embarrassed in a kick-your-toes-into-the-carpet sort of way, I shook my head no. I also thought she'd commiserate with me. Isn't the ability to operate a remote control a guy thing?

My brother-in-law chortled. "Neither can I. But I really don't care all that much. If I can't figure it out, I can always go read a book."

"Me too," I exhaled. Bill is a pretty smart guy, so maybe I wasn't as dumb as I felt.

That's when I realized that knowing how to operate a remote control isn't limited to the male of the species. But it is genetic.

There are times I wish I knew how to turn on the TV, but more often I pine for our very first set, the one we purchased in 1983. It had a nineteen-inch screen and push buttons that made the picture appear. A dial changed channels with a satisfying click. You knew you were accomplishing something with each rotation. It was a color TV — a washed-out, faded blue jean sort of color — and pre-satellite TV, it was equally sincere in the availability of programs. Some stations were fuzzier than others, but unless you could successfully position its rabbit ears to divine the frequency source, you put up with it. It just was.

And there was no remote control.

As the years unfurled, Dr. K discovered methods of circumventing the TV stations, for multiplying viewing possibilities, and resources to incorporate computers into the viewing experience. What used to be a method for relaxation had become a nerve-wracking recitation of steps, ones that weren't guaranteed to work — even for him. What had once been enjoyable was now an exercise fraught with anxiety. We have missed many a Super Bowl, Oscar awards extravaganza, presidential debate, and the odd Saturday movie night, simply because even he couldn't figure it out.

Bill was faced with the same dilemma. My sister-in-law Sarah had taken an older laptop, and to Bill and my minds, jerry-rigged it to perform the same functions as had my friendly, old nineteen-inch TV.

"She told me to hit Command Q and step away from the device — because it's not a computer anymore! And under no circumstances close the lid!"

Because what might happen? For all Bill and I (and those of our limited capabilities) knew, if you closed the lid the device might explode. Crazier things have happened. Look at the Samsung Galaxy Note 7.

Like Sarah, Dr. K provides instructions, rattling them off quickly as I hold the remote, an alien thing in the palm of my hand having no connection to common sense. I poke at the box in growing distress — the round button on the upper left, the dial in the middle, the rocker on the right, a succession of nonlinear steps for what is supposed to be an escape from daily tasks. I'll happily absorb and regurgitate seemingly trivial words, concepts, and ideas, but when I try to decode the finicky steps dictated by my husband for remote control usage, it is no better than grasping at sand running through a sieve.

The thing about a remote control is, whoever holds one in the palm of their hand is King of the World.

It's a potent thing to relinquish.

Remote controls are frustrating because, ultimately, they are a surrogate for ourselves and our abilities. They are a tangible demonstration that there is much in life over which we can exert no influence.

I used to think it would be nice to have a remote control to keep life tethered. It wouldn't be to dominate others or to control the world, although an on/off button might be pretty cool. It would be reassuring to have small measures to guarantee life is exactly how I want it to be.

But I've come to realize life is uncontrollable. That's what keeps it interesting, annoying as hell, and anything other than plain vanilla.

IMMIGRANT LIFE: TAKING OFF THE CONE OF SHAME

NOVEMBER 4, 2016

When my South Korean daughter-in-law and my son adopted a puppy, I created a story about what my daughter-in-law told me she felt like as an immigrant in America — in the words of a puppy.

My name is Moro. I am a Shiba Inu puppy. I want to tell you my story.

If you're unfamiliar with my breed, I'm petite, originally from Japan, very fastidious, and have a feisty personality. But I don't want to tell you too much. I'm afraid you'll pass judgment because I am not a dog breed you know. I worry that you might label me or put me in a category.

I am not a Golden retriever. I am not an English sheepdog. Although my name sounds similar, I am not Toto, the Cairn terrier, the dog who was immortalized in *The Wizard of Oz*. The American Kennel Club only recognized my breed in 1992.

So who am I? I am Moro the Shiba Inu, all of one foot tall! I am fierce! When I growl and bare my teeth, my black and white fur bristles and stands up straight! My ancestors protected samurai warrior families when they left home for battle.

These days, there are no samurai warriors. And I have never lived in Japan.

But when I was adopted and moved from the Pennsylvania farm where I was born to big city America, I moved to a place where I couldn't understand what people were saying.

On my Pennsylvania farm, there was a dirty farmhouse, with comfy, squishy humans who didn't talk much. I romped with my brothers and sisters in fields where tall grass waved. When the sun sank behind the hills, I curled up next to the other puppies in sweet-smelling hay, lulled to sleep with dreams of where we would play tomorrow.

On the farm, there were other animals that weren't like me and my siblings. Some made mooing noises and others whinnied and snorted a lot. And there were some animals that didn't eat like the rest of us. They ate liquid and breathed out smoke. They were noisier than all of my brothers and sisters barking at once. But mostly, the farm was a quiet place.

I could have lived on my farm forever, but one morning everything changed.

Three humans who talked fast knocked on the farmhouse door. My humans told me, "They have come to adopt you."

I didn't know the word 'adopt'. But I sniffed their hands and they smoothed my fur.

And then they stuffed me into a dark crate lined with soft padding. They put me into one of the animals that eats liquid and we bumped away from my farm! I craned my neck to see my brothers and sisters so I could bark goodbye   but I could only see darkness.

I wondered if I would ever cuddle with them again.

These new humans talked so much! They sounded like my brothers and sisters barking all at once. They talked about our journey in cars and trains. They talked about big city life.

Traveling to big city in cars and trains made me wobbly and woozy.

I learned there are cars called 'taxis' that dodge through a sea of cars in darkness. Taxis are the noisiest of all. They weave through traffic and make horns blare and sirens whine.

These new humans live in a tiny apartment touching the sky. I run around it like a crazy dog. I miss the green, rolling hills on my farm.

The humans call me the 'Shiba 500' because I race and chase around the tiny apartment. I dodge the couch, bump the table legs, and zoom into the kitchen for the final turn.

When I knocked over dinner on the table, the humans took me to play with other dogs in the dog park.

We stand on tiny strips of grass. I greet the other dogs and say "Konbanwa", but they don't understand I am wishing them "Good evening" in Japanese. So instead, the German shepherd and I race and chase on pavement. The French poodle and I sniff each other daintily. And the tiny Chihuahua watches us play, his round, black eyes shimmering. He shivers as the cold wind whips up from the river.

I am lonely and sad. I miss my old farm, where I understood the dogs and humans.

I try to understand big city language, but the humans talk so much and ask so many questions. Questions on the street. Questions in the store. Questions on the bus. Where I come from, strangers don't ask questions. In big city they call it 'making small talk', but it makes me anxious.

Being a new dog breed in big city America, you probably think I talk funny, no matter how much I try to get it right.

I am sad when my words are misunderstood. I have to curl into a ball to calm down.

When the humans aren't looking, I study their faces and how they talk with each other. I imitate what their faces do when they speak. I keep practicing and someday, I think they'll understand what I'm trying to tell them.

Big city rules are hard to understand, too.

One day the humans told me because I was adopted, I had to go to the vet to have surgery to get fixed.

Was I broken?

I licked my four paws and nibbled my one tail. All were there! I scratched behind each ear with one hind leg. Two ears! What was wrong with me?

But they took me to the vet and I stood on a high table in a cold, white room. I didn't want to look over the edge. What if I fell into the abyss and could never return? What if the abyss was dark like the crate on the train? Or the sirens never stopped? I think about that and shiver, even in my dreams.

The vet pushed her hands on my tummy and announced, "Time for surgery!"

I became very woozy and when I woke up, I was wearing the plastic cone of shame.

I have never seen a human wearing a cone of shame. Have you? Was the cone a sign I could never be fixed? Did I have to wear it because I was adopted?

It wasn't dark inside the cone but I could only see straight ahead. I tripped on it when I walked. I couldn't eat, couldn't sleep, and I drooled all over the plastic. Worst of all, I couldn't growl and bare my teeth. My black and white fur was sticky. I felt sad and not fierce at all.

The humans asked me several times a day how I felt. I wanted to tell them I felt different and sad. But all they wanted to hear was, "I'm fine."

It was probably safest to tell them that because if I told them the truth, they might take me back to the cold, white place and put me back up on the high table.

I felt singled out and different.

The humans tried to make me happy, but I wondered, during that awful week I wore the cone of shame, if they did it to remind me that I'm not a human, that they don't always understand me and perhaps never completely will?

But then, one of my humans wrapped me in his yellow baby blanket. It smelled nice; it smelled of him. It was warm and cuddly like my brothers and sisters.

The next day, my humans stuffed me into the dark crate and we took a ride on the subway, all the way back to the vet. They made me stand on the high table in the cold, white room.

But this day was different!

The vet took off the cone of shame, pushed her hands on my tummy, and told me I was good to go! I licked her hand and gazed into her eyes.

We returned home to our tiny apartment that touches the sky and my humans dressed me in a samurai warrior costume. I growled and bared my teeth at them. They laughed and smoothed my bristling fur.

I licked their hands. And then we curled up on the couch together and snuggled.

I'll keep watching, listening, learning, thinking. And someday, my humans won't think of me as different. I will be one with them.

UP THE CREEK WITH A PADDLE

DECEMBER 2, 2016

Heroes and the villains they battle define how we see the world, in story, in myth, and everyday life. But there needs to be balance. Humor is the way.

As a novelist, anger and despair — and we might as well throw in angst, drama, and life itself — all of that stuff bumps me into storytelling mode. When I read the newspaper these days, or Facebook and Twitter, it's evident. I get the sense we are dealing with the Dark Side, the Forces of Evil, He-Who-Must-Not-Be-Named. Pick your villain. There are a lot of life-sized role models out there from which to choose.

One of the best methods of understanding and defining the forces of good and evil is by looking at the writings of Joseph Campbell, author of the iconic *The Hero with a Thousand Faces*. We are all heroes in some way, and we all find ourselves at some point going up the creek without a paddle. That's also called 'the struggle'.

A successful hero needs resilience. There are a number of steps to wade through on any journey to achieve the ultimate goal, whether it be saving the world or buying a friend a bag of Hershey's kisses to console a bruised heart.

A hero is someone whose actions are beyond the normal range of everyday experience, and the hero gives something of herself in the process.

We can all be everyday heroes, once we are willing to become empowered with the knowledge of life and all its permutations. And life, the mirror of myth, is made up of elements both comic and tragic.

But I've decided I'm not going up the creek unless I bring a paddle with me.

You may be thinking, *Hey, Emily. You're not understanding the metaphor. You're supposed to be up the creek without the paddle, because that's why you're in the mess you're in at the moment.*

As with the ultimate goal — or prize — messes come in all shapes and sizes. There are political messes, there are financial messes, and then there are the intensely painful personal messes, the ones that pull your innards out through your esophagus, leaving you drained, gasping for air and wondering if tomorrow is worth living for.

But we all have a paddle. It's hidden inside each and every person.

The paddle is laughter: the ability to find humor in a situation, the ability to turn the putrid into a pun, and most importantly, the ability to laugh loudest at yourself.

Case in point: a friend and I were waxing philosophical about the results of the — I almost hate to type the word lest it jinx this post, but what the hell — the election. Yes. That.

We were, as are thousands of others right now, comparing certain politicians and outcomes to Adolf Hitler (another potential post jinxed, but I'm on a roll now). I told my friend I'd noticed my iPhone autocorrect refused to capitalize the name 'Hitler'. Clearly, there were evil forces afoot.

As a mathematician, the potential for calculating odds was too great a lure, and he set out to put my hypothesis to the test. Instead of sinking further into a reverie of loamy gloom, the where are we going? what will we do next? how will the world ever survive — in short, how most people were responding to the electoral shake-up on social media, including throw-up emoticons — he entered a few queries on Microsoft Word to see what automatically capitalized and what didn't. In other words, while over fifty percent of Americans held their heads in their hands, he went to work to solve the problem.

To whit:

What is hitler's first name? when did adolf hitler die? Who is orval fauns? When did jack benny die? What is George patton famous for? Who shot hitler? who shot mary? How did lee Harvey Oswald die? What did roy rogers name his horse?

The answer is 'Trigger', of course, to that last one, and probably the only one most of you out there in internet-land would know off the top of your head. And while it proved that hitler was never capitalized, neither were a lot of other formal names.

Even so, that bunch of questions, and the only pop culture answer I could contribute triggered a solution for my current angst.

We need to take things a whole lot less seriously. And get this: it's possible there is no ulterior motive.

This doesn't mean I'll sit idly by, floating up to the ceiling with laughter in the manner of *Mary Poppins'* Uncle Albert.

But it does mean that I won't engage in behavior and activities which are futile, the ones which only make me angrier. It's futile to banter back-and-forth on Facebook with trolls who hop onto threads with my friends, their only purpose to stoke the fire, their only purpose to insult me with comments I now prize for their comedic value. Like the one where they suggested I *'go back to reading Astrology and let the adults run the world.'* It was particularly inventive since I didn't know these people from Adam and wondered how they knew I can't begin the day without reading the horoscopes in the daily newspaper. Their insight was astonishing. But they neglected to mention that I've also read *The Federalist Papers* cover to cover six times, too. In that, they really have no idea who I am.

But we need balance. We need the people who read both palms and respectable history — a history that has, over the last 240 years (and still counting) been proven to work.

I will also not sit idly by and let bigotry, racism, and infringement on personal rights protected by our country's constitution and laws undermine the social tenets that form the bedrock of this country, whether that infringement is by people I know acting out towards people I consider family or friends, or whether they are the acts of strangers upon strangers.

There's something that feels good about doing what's right. There's also something about holding others accountable for their actions and words. There is no free pass to hurt another being. I hope there will be others of you who agree with this and take a stand.

It Starts with a Fish

We also need to get a grip: the world is not going to end tomorrow. There is no Death Star pointed at Earth, guided by a clinically depressed man masked and dressed in black with a chronic case of the grudges, one who always saw the glass as half empty. There are no flying monkeys in the sky, (spoiler alert) the Wicked Witch is dead, and all that's left is a melted puddle of evil. Voldemort (oops, the name just slipped out) is also dead, because of wand operator error. If these aren't evildoers with whom you're familiar, make a list of your own. It never hurts to add to the watch list.

And while you're at it, add a list of heroes alongside. We might find the heroes outweigh the bad guys in the long run. The world can only handle a certain number of evildoers.

I may run this by my mathematician friend and see what the odds are. And then we can laugh at the silliness of it.

PINK HATS, DARNED RATS, AND PAYING THE PIPER

FEBRUARY 3, 2017

An awakening of sorts, a day made meaningful because of a silly pink hat.

Saturday, January 21, 2017 was bookended by time spent in bars in San Francisco. Regardless of the side of the aisle on which you sit, it was probably a fitting activity for the day after Donald Trump's inauguration. For me, it was more than simply having a drink or four because for five hours during the middle of that long day of January 21, I wore a pink knitted hat — yes, one of those, the now infamous ones.

As a writer — an artist of sorts, I guess — I often find myself adrift in the sea of my mind. Following a train of thought, a word, concept or musical phrase, artists get caught up in the whorls and eddies, allowing them to suck us in and lead us to the truth, whether it be a sentence, a paragraph, a symphony, or nirvana.

I also talk myself into doing things I possibly shouldn't and maybe oughtn't, simply for the sake of experience. You can't write it if you haven't smelled the surroundings.

You have to start with facts, which in this case was a presidential election that took the nation by surprise.

That's how I started off with plans to join college friends in Washington, D.C. for the Women's March. It sounded so progressive, a chance to take society's temperature. I'd get up bright and early (2 am) to drive to the airport and catch my 6:30 am flight to Baltimore. We'd have a college reunion of sorts (with group hugs and singing),

153

hop on public transportation to D.C. bright and early Saturday morning, go march and sing with the others along the Mall, sightsee the Washington Monument along the way, climb back onto public transportation to Baltimore, and eventually make it back to Colorado late Sunday night.

It all sounded breathlessly exciting, until I thought about it some more because:

- I was drowning in work
- It's cold in January in D.C.
- I hate to get up that early, unless I'm going skiing — and even then, not so much
- I have this *thing* about being in crowds

The more I thought about it, in a becoming mired in quicksand way of thinking, the more I couldn't. The trip occupied me day and night — I obsessed — and finally, embarrassed, admitted to myself and my friends it wasn't going to happen. I hated me.

I decided to travel, as originally planned that weekend, to accompany Dr. K to a medical conference in San Francisco. I could work, he could work, the obsessive-compulsive in my head would be happy.

But then another friend offered to knit me a pink hat. A pink pussy hat, to be exact. It was her contribution to the cause.

I thanked her but explained I was going to be in San Francisco instead, that I had a crowd problem. She suggested I could wear the hat in the hotel room.

I was beginning to sound ridiculous, even to myself. I have no problem speaking to crowds. Why couldn't I be in one? So I signed up for the march in San Francisco. How big could that possibly be, I reasoned? And it would certainly be warmer than Washington in January.

You have to realize, I'm a Jewish American Princess — and although I'm not of the practicing sort of Jewishness, there is still a cultural identity. Celebrating Hanukkah. Getting the manicures. Making dinner reservations. I have a classical music and jazz bent. We JAPs can become a joke of ourselves. We tend to voice opinions, but not too loudly. Firm but not aggressive; we try to make friends with everyone. We are Jewish, but more than that, we are Americans. We want to fit into our surroundings because of the stories we've heard again and again from our parents, those who left much behind in Nazi Germany and other European countries.

I had friends who were pleased I was going to march — that I was breaking out of JAP-dom to speak up — and a few were equally astonished by it. "The pink hats," they sputtered. "You *do* know what they represent? They're so dirty…"

The morning of the march dawned on a drizzly San Francisco. Dr. K asked if I'd like to go out for lunch and I declined, explaining I had to work.

And then I changed my mind. It was becoming a common theme associated with the happenings of January 21, 2017.

An elevator whisked us up to a crowded dim sum restaurant where an elegantly dressed Chinese woman asked if we had reservations. I looked down at my ragged jeans and tennis shoes. Clothed for the march, it was obvious I didn't fit in, and I began to feel uncomfortable. At that moment, I was as un-JAP-like as could be.

"We can seat you at the bar," she said, her voice lilting and musical, and she gestured to a stretch of glowing cobalt blue glass where lights twinkled, illuminating crystal bottles in immaculate rows. I was beginning to float; it was the surroundings, it was the perfumed air, both floral and subtle Asian spice, it was the lack of judgment from the hostess. We were welcome, no matter what we were wearing.

Two fruity, orchid-adorned cocktails later, still feeling lulled and surreal, we strolled back to the hotel for a quick nap. Dr. K could head back to his conference, and I would brave the crowds. The pavement was already dotted with groups of women, many dressed in pink, many sporting pink, knitted hats. Passersby looked, pointed, comments were discretely made. Market Street hummed with unseen energy.

Back in the room, I popped on the pink hat and evaluated which layers to wear; the rain, as predicted, was beginning to fall.

"I think I'll go along," Dr. K said, deciding to skip the afternoon conference sessions.

As we walked quickly up Market Street towards the Civic Center, the trickle of people became a steady flow, then a river, then an ocean of humanity. Our steps were slowed by the numbers but not the rain.

I had never been surrounded by so many others. Women, men, children, families — of all ages, races, interests, and diversities. We stood in the rain and talked with each other before the rally began. We noted the signs people carried, often laughing at the humor. We clustered, we nudged, we encouraged, we learned about each other.

We stood as individuals with particular wishes and interests, we stood together as a group resolved to right wrongs and promote individual freedoms — a mass of Americana — because that's what this country is. So many differences, so much uniqueness, and yet so much willingness to acknowledge the sameness.

Five hours later, soaked and chilled, Dr. K and I returned to the hotel to warm up with hot baths before we changed for dinner. Given the ongoing crush of people, the reservations I'd made for a restaurant only half a mile away were impossible to reach, even by foot, so sans pink hat, we walked downstairs to the hotel bar, hoping for a table.

In Maxfield's Pied Piper Bar, vestiges of the past are notable in the ornately gilded wood paneling, crystal chandeliers and comfy, green leather chairs pulled up to tables. Maxfield Parrish's original painting, *The Pied Piper*, glows across its sixteen-foot length, where on the canvas children caper and dance behind the colorful clown leading them to lives unknown. There is a legend, a tale told and passed down from events recorded in 1284 in the German town of Hamelin: a successful rat catcher whose fees went unpaid by the town extracted cruel retribution when he whisked away 130 Hamelin children forever. The painting is honored and esteemed, reflecting San Francisco's heritage not so much because it lectures; more so because it acknowledges human foibles, weaknesses, and folly.

That night of January 21, the normally staid bar was packed to the walls, abuzz with talk of the march, the community, the feelings of inclusion it had engendered. Drinks were ordered, smiles flashed between strangers.

The day was made meaningful because of a silly pink hat.

With the recent turn of events politically and even socially, I've become more outspoken in my opinions. As a writer, I express thoughts in novels and on this blog. But I perform factual research first.

I used to worry about what people thought. I've come to realize it's more dangerous to suppress truth. I write stories, trying to make sense of the world, to take its mental temperature and hopefully teach that in the long run, it's human kindness and decency that wins and is remembered with favor.

'Paying the piper' is a euphemism for paying a high price for something deemed unfair, that when not paid can end up with dire consequences. We all end up paying the piper for something, whether it be in children lost, momentum redirected, attitudes changed, or self-identification taking a different track.

I probably won't put on that pink hat again, but the experience of wearing it and joining with others will stay with me. Life turned a corner that day out on the streets of San Francisco and it's time to move forward and speak up.

But I'll still be making reservations for dinner.

I HAVEN'T WRITTEN THAT BOOK YET

MARCH 3, 2017

I always wanted to write a book about my heritage. I haven't written it yet, but my second novel was released last week. Here's a bit about the #amwriting life.

I always thought it would be fun to write a book. I was sure of the topic — it would be the story of my heritage, stemming from my status as a first-generation American. It would be the story of how my family ended up in the United States.

I have yet to write that book. But last week I celebrated the release of my second novel, *Drinking the Knock Water*. Its theme came to me while on a tour of the Hudson River as we drew near the Statue of Liberty at dusk. So, while it isn't exactly what I expected my first or second novel to be about, it was emotionally driven by my impression of the statue, glowing white, torch raised high, surrounded by a churn of dark waters.

Born of that statuesque vision, one that took my breath away, *Drinking the Knock Water* developed legs after visiting the historic Sleepy Hollow Cemetery — the very one where Washington Irving's Headless Horseman raged. And while I used the town of Sleepy Hollow and its surroundings for inspiration, I didn't want to write a thriller or chiller. Based on a theme of infertility, I wanted to tell a story about people who experience loss and disconnection with the world.

Growing up, one of my fondest memories is of my friend Kim and I biking to the library, empty backpacks slung over our shoulders. After an hour spent roaming the stacks, we'd cycle home, each loaded down with, on average, ten books. Gleefully, we would retreat to one or the other of our bedrooms (we lived on the same block, so we alternated turns), where for hours the two of us sat on the floor in silence reading our treasure trove. No conversation occurred or was needed. On cooler summer days we read stretched out on the trampoline in Kim's backyard.

One by one, the books were devoured and then returned to the library for a new cache each week.

Oh so boring, you say? Perhaps for some, but for Kim and me, the hours spent delving into the imagination of others was priceless.

Fast forward, through history and law degrees, and nearly five years practicing law. Two kids followed, along with my husband's medical practice, which I managed in between making hot chocolate on demand while attaining the status of picture-perfect field trip mom.

That book had still not been written.

Oh, I tried several times. I pulled out a yellow legal pad and began penning a story I was certain was worthwhile to tell. But that was all I did. There were no notes or outlines. There was no research into the history of Nazi Germany, and its forced relocation of peoples who understood they were fortunate to have escaped certain death from the hydrogen cyanide-based pesticide Zyklon B, the experimental gas at concentration camps Nazis selected to use on their 'pests'.

But in short, my writing had no organization or method. I mourned the fact that I could have been an author.

When I turned forty, I was invited to join a women's club in my town, one known for imposing rigorous research topics on its members. After spending hours reading, researching, and writing lengthy papers on topics often not of our choosing, we read the papers aloud to the club, presenting PowerPoints with pretty — and sometimes gritty — pictures.

As an attorney, I knew how to track down a footnote to the nth degree to find the answer that could win a written argument on its merits. But I had never learned how to research to tell a story.

After I'd been a member for several years, I was assigned a paper about Joseph Campbell, author of *The Hero's Journey,* and his millennium-spanning anthropological analysis of cultural similarities in storytelling around the globe. I began to understand the complicated process of getting your point across in prose.

And so I began writing my first novel.

I learned that a novel plants a seed of truth, and from there, roots burrow down into its soil, growing and developing buds as the story evolves and blossoms. If the roots are good and the soil is fertile, with regular treatments of fertilizer and water a story will continue to bud, bloom, and share its beautiful perfume.

I learned that I needed to see the stage I set the story on in person, I needed to smell the surroundings. That's the only way to make words seem real.

I don't want to bore you with a regurgitation of the hows and whatnots of novel-writing. You don't want to know about the time spent mulling over the spelling of a word, its etymological history, the variations of synonyms, and why understanding a word's antonym can open a Pandora's Box of meanings.

You aren't interested in the time lost in thought as I track a concept, drowning in the Google sea of thoughts, ideas, numbers, and lessons. Or the 3 am ideas that wake me up, or the stop-in-mid-sentence dinner conversations with Dr. K, the ones where I interrupt him, saying, "Wait, wait, wait — I need to write down what you just said."

You aren't interested in the late-night dinners, or the dinners that never got cooked and we ordered take-out in exhaustion. Or the brain-drain of finishing a chapter or sometimes only a thought, how it leaves my mind numb, unable to hitch two words together to speak aloud. There are the days when I tell myself I'll write three pages, but only finish one new sentence. Or the number of times I edit a novel before it finally gets the go-ahead — it's thirty, all told.

And I still panic. Particularly when the characters I've created wake me up in the middle of the night insisting that the storyline would be better if it went in this direction (or that) and they whisper words, words that jolt me awake from my dreams to make sure I capture them in notes erratically typed on my cell phone in the dark.

So, let's re-write that entire scene, Emily, my characters whisper in my mind as I sleep. Even though you're not supposed to keep your cell phone on the bedside table.

There are the lunch dates skipped, the friends who just don't get why all I do is sit at my desk and stare at a computer screen, wishing for the words to come. Any word. Please, just one to get the flow moving.

And the friends who ask, "Where have you been lately? I haven't seen you in forever!"

Most frightening of all, there are the what-ifs. The fear that once you, the author, open your head up to the world, allowing all to see what goes on inside there. Well then. What will the world think of you?

But there is also freedom. Once a thought is processed and written, whether on my blog or a point in a novel, it makes space for more thoughts, more creativity, more ability to stretch my mind in new directions.

But telling you all of this would be boring — like listening to your car mechanic tell you the step-by-step process of how he recalibrated your brakes. You're just happy the car comes to a full stop.

You're happy there are good books to read. As am I. And I'm equally happy to write them.

THE HOW TO MOTHER-IN-LAW OPERATIONS MANUAL

JULY 7, 2017

Becoming a mother-in-law requires an operations manual if you want to have a good relationship with your new daughter-in-law.

I was recently gifted another kid.

It was a great opportunity to add a child to our family without me being pregnant, which previously (twice) has meant gaining fifty pounds a pop. Thanks to my son, I've become a mother-in-law.

As everyone knows, marriage is a battle.

At least, that's what all the self-help books tell us. Relationships between men and women are called the battle of the sexes. Presumably, if you believe what these books say, when you hook up with someone for life you are headed for a lifelong war zone.

I think there are two war zones when families combine, and it has nothing to do with either the sexes, or sex, which is more of a problem-solver.

The first zone is raising children from birth forward. By acquiring my third child via marriage, it eliminated not only pregnancy, but Teenage Mouth Syndrome and the 'What am I?!' years in one fell swoop.

However, the marriage of my firstborn did plunge me directly into the depths of mother-in-lawhood, a state of alternate reality. I've relied on those who have walked the path before me for sage advice in this most critical second war zone.

To a one, my friends told me to kiss my son goodbye if I were to cross swords with my new daughter-in-law, recognizing that she was now his queen and commander-in-chief. It was highly recommended that I learn to follow the mantra: keep your mouth shut.

I thought this over for a while — okay, maybe a minute or two — before coming to the understanding that this is very difficult. One minute your son is a needy child, phoning for advice and psychotherapy, the next he's sleeping with another woman and going out to brunch with her.

The bed issue was never a problem; it was breakfast that dealt me the final blow.

But if we can agree that marriage is supposed to be a battle, there needs to be a manual of tactical maneuvers.

On a recent tour of the USS Becuna, a World War II submarine permanently parked dockside at Penn's Landing in Philadelphia, I spotted an embossing tape list tacked on the stainless-steel bulkhead of the submarine. The list provides a great jumping off point for a mother-in-law operations manual.

1. Rig for Dive/Rig for Surface:

This is the crucial moment when you realize your son is in love with someone other than you. Your heart plummets, dropping to the ocean bed — or however far down World War II submarines can dive — before slowly regaining elevation. It's an ethereal experience. You're deadweight. But then, suddenly filled with buoyancy, capital letters zoom through your head in ecstasy: OMGOMGOMG! He's actually gone and caught one!

2. Fire:

Your heart's afire, your brain's afire, your credit card is melted plastic. Before you know it, you've promised assistance in whatever way your new child wants to help create the most perfect wedding ever! From 1,700 miles away. Yay.

Google Maps advises two things:

- This route has tolls.
- Your destination is in a different time zone. Two, to be exact.

3. Emergency Ventilation:

You take efforts to discover who this person is who has stolen your son away forever. Rationalization sets in. He's a fairly decent person at this stage of his life. Therefore, she must have similar, admirable qualities. You tentatively include her in family group texts, worried about overstepping bounds, leery about seeming too pushy.

- You discover a mutual love of dogs and French fruit tarts.

4. Collision/Flooding:

As you trade Pinterest pictures, visions of wedding gowns and floral arrangements collide. Will the differences of style sink the submarine before launch? She's minimalist, you're a fluffy bouffant of lace and tulle.

- You discover a mutual affection for oysters on the half shell and wild flowers.

5. Toxic Gas:

She texts you at 8 o'clock on a wintery evening, requesting addresses for the names you've provided for the wedding list. She wants them NOW. According to the Wedding Planning Manual, the invitations will be late if they are mailed yesterday. You stay up until eleven that night and send them off, including detailed instructions for how-to-address-the-inside-envelopes for each invitee. Emily Post is riding shotgun.

- You realize on receiving your invitation that she had no intention of using inside envelopes.
- It's a new generation, Mom. The invitations are quite casual. Quite.
- You realize you received an invitation to the wedding.

6. Passive Defense:

Months pass, wedding plans are on autopilot, and you drift. It's time to let the couple be — to a point. Periodic spurts of texts erupt, there are phone calls of distress. The instruction sheet for the caterer has been filled out and forgotten. They are a couple; they have their lives, you have yours.

- Your son and daughter-in-law take a week's vacation but send you pics of their meals, unasked. As a food photographer, you're pretty darned thrilled.
- You discover a mutual love of Instagram, food shots, and cooking.

7. Air Revitalization:

On an impromptu visit to their home in New York City, as you head out for an after dinner walk to the dog park on the edge of the East River, your daughter-in-law hands you the leash of their dog.

8. Depth Charge/Deep Submergence:

She texts or calls occasionally for advice. You begin to understand you've added an Insta-grownup to the family, but she still listens to you, the adult. Sometimes.

9. Silent Running:

You learn that her favorite nonverbal way to communicate is by texting you GIFs. You learn how to search out GIFs on the internet, copy, paste, and respond in kind.

- You see that your daughter-in-law has a fantastic sense of humor.
- You understand why your son fell in love with her like he was hit by a ton of bricks.

10. Repel Boarders/Sneak Attack:

A struggle ensues as stragglers RSVP to the wedding invitations, as your daughter-in-law freaks out with seating arrangements for the reception, as the meaning of "Répondez s'il vous plaît" is rendered meaningless by twenty-first-century manners. The battle of the families resurfaces. You placate with, "Everyone understands how to respond to an invitation differently," knowing this is a meaningless platitude, and silently are in complete agreement with her.

- Sigh.

11. Rescue and Assistance/Hand Dive/Cold Weather Snorkel:

You arrive early at the wedding venue to tuck and polish. You commiserate and make light of the fact that she forgot the wedding dress in their New York City apartment and needs to turn around and drive back two hours to retrieve it, ascribing it to nerves. You learn how to create a bridal bouquet. The wild flowers are already wilting from the summer heat but you tuck the bouquet into the wine fridge in the bed and breakfast, hoping for the best.

- Your daughter-in-law declares the bridal bouquet perfect — exactly what she wanted, in fact.
- Sigh. Of. Relief.
- Your hair a frizzed-out mess, after a quick shower you don your very-much-a-mother-in-law dress, wondering why there is so much humidity in the middle of Pennsylvania in June in the summer. And then you realize the futility of considering

humidity in June in the middle of Pennsylvania. And you go on with the show.

12. OBA Operating Instructions:

Later in the evening, observing happy wedding guests — the family from both sides who've traveled across the globe to celebrate and your son's friends dating all the way back to grade school and forward — you remember his Bar Mitzvah at age thirteen. True to tradition, all from the Rabbi down informed him he was now a man.

But when my son married, my new daughter-in-law made him a human being.

I tell her that a lot. In texts, in GIFs. In person.

She says I'm giving her too much credit. I don't think so.

FIREFLIES LIGHT THE PATH SO WE CAN RUN WITH SCISSORS

AUGUST 4, 2017

In the darkened parks of historic Philadelphia, it seemed as if those who founded our country walked with us. Fireflies lit our path, illuminating history.

I have a sister who is very wise, wiser than her years, perhaps. She's younger than me, but knows a lot when it comes to common sense.

In her wisdom, she only makes suggestions about two things. The first is to remind me to bring non-dairy creamer to our monthly breakfast since our favorite spot doesn't offer it. With my dairy allergy, I try to avoid milk whenever possible.

The second thing is she tells me not to run with scissors. I remember to bring the non-dairy creamer about half the time. I tend to run with scissors much more often.

An example of this is when I asked Dr. K if I could write a blog post about politics. He cringed and said, "I think it would be better if you wrote about dogs."

I told him I would write about fireflies instead. He thought fireflies were a safe topic, but I explained it's running with scissors of a different sort.

The firefly idea occurred to me when my sister texted me the morning of our monthly breakfast date.

Michelle: *Did you leave me a voicemail message on my home number? The message sounded kind of like you but I couldn't understand a word of it.*

Me: *I didn't. Was it asking for a ransom because I'd been kidnapped, or was it begging you to buy health insurance because the world is going to hell in a handbasket?*

What's interesting about this interchange is this: my sister never texts. She hardly ever turns on her cell phone. But the world today has rattled her enough to double-check on me.

I don't know about you, but I get a lot of phone calls these days I ignore. They're from unrecognizable numbers and they're from area codes all over the country. Cincinnati, Palo Alto, Saint Petersburg (Florida, not Russia) and Atlanta — all from places where I don't know anyone, and if I did, they'd most likely message me on Facebook or have my email. They are strangers calling from a strange land.

Sometimes I listen to the pleas, the insistent requests to call about what is soon to be lost, but most of the time I don't accept the call. Instead, I watch and worry about a political landscape where people cannot talk with each other about how to govern our country. We cannot share concerns or address our differences in a rational manner without being offensive. We suddenly live in a country where people are arrested for speaking out and speaking up.

Most of us were raised on the mantra that it's impolite to talk about politics and religion. I've had friends and family hemorrhage from my life over these topics — and yet, a recent visit to Philadelphia illuminated the situation in which our country now finds itself in the most microscopic of ways.

I decided I could run with scissors because of the fireflies.

I am a historian, more than anything else. At registration in college — back in the days where you had to show up and register in person the week before classes began — my plan had been to major in psychology. That plan backfired when I learned Psych 101 was already full. What to do next?

I decided then and there on the cold concrete floor of Folsom Field House at the University of Colorado that I would follow my next love — history. But the study of the intricate workings and oddities of the human mind has always played a part in my studies.

For a historian, visiting Philadelphia is the equivalent of The Mall of America for a shopaholic.

We arrived and set out to explore the one square mile of near-sacred land that carries more historical significance than any other mile anywhere in the United States.

We wandered the streets, stopping to visit Congress Hall, Carpenters' Hall, Old City Hall, and the Second Bank of the United States. There was Declaration House, Franklin Court — Ben Franklin's hangout, with his own museum to house a few of his inventions — and the Betsy Ross House. Standing in line to see the Liberty Bell was the most time-consuming. It ate up nearly thirty minutes of tourism.

And then there was Independence Hall — where a handful of traitors declared independence from a tyrannical king, one who happened to be the most powerful man in the world at the time. Independence Hall is stark and unassuming. Spare, green-clothed tables line the room where the greatest democratic experiment in the history of the world began. It's the room where the United States Constitution was drafted. The tour cost a $1 ticket, wait-time thirty minutes tops.

Along with nooks and crannies to explore on Philadelphia's cobblestone streets, the most expensive viewing opportunity in town was the sparkling new Museum of the American Revolution. At 19 bucks a pop, I wondered what marvels it might hold, but went with the flow and bought tickets.

In a darkened auditorium, a movie entitled *Washington's War Tent* was shown. The film told the story of the American Revolution, the difficulties endured by the Continental Army, the suffering of those left at home to tend farms and town businesses. And the overarching worry that loved ones would be strung up as traitors to king and country. Then the movie screen rolled away to reveal a canvas field tent.

General Washington, our country's first president, spent the war years with his troops. From 1778-1783, Washington slept and planned tactical maneuvers protected by the tent's canvas walls. It's often called the First Oval Office.

It was this simplicity which most struck me about the buildings where the Founding Fathers dreamt up a New World, one based on freedom and equality. No one was too grand to talk to anyone else. Farmers, planters, and businessmen strove together with a common purpose. They represented different life and business philosophies. The taint of slavery hung over all their heads, an ugliness no one was willing to address at face value, instead passing the problem down to future generations.

All were traitors to the king and the English Parliament, and yet they risked their personal freedoms, working inside these plain buildings furnished with hard wooden chairs. There was no gilding or rich tapestry. The workspaces served a purpose to discuss and write their intentions.

It seemed we walked in their footsteps each night after dinner along Philadelphia's cobblestoned streets. The historic places and homes are lit by modern means, but in the verdant, brick-walled parks the flickering of fireflies welcomed us. It was only a few days until the Fourth of July, when, 241 years ago, steps for independence were taken. Perhaps this is why in the darkened parks we felt the breath of these early Americans on our cheeks, as if somehow they strode silently alongside us.

In the parks, fireflies danced in luminescence, their bodies creating light from a chemical reaction, balancing science and magic.

Most strikingly, there are no fences within that square mile of American history, save a low gate stretching across the entrance to Independence Hall. A few National Park rangers stand guard, reserved and subtle, but they smile more than the guards at Buckingham Palace. Visitors traverse the area around the buildings without boundaries, exploring, touching brick and wooden walls, encountering the same sensations as did those people who walked the same Philadelphia cobblestones over two hundred years ago. I'll bet they saw fireflies, too.

It's this openness that is remarkable about these near sacred grounds in central Philadelphia. It sends a message to the world. Given their significance, it's notable how small the buildings are. In them, processes were established, creating an enormous test of whether government can be created by the people, for the people.

The firefly dances flicker and shine, urging us today to run with scissors, as did those who walked before us.

And in the openness of the walkways, there is an unspoken message that the intentions of our visionaries will endure.

That too, is common sense.

PLAYING THE GAME OF MARRIED LIFE FOR THIRTY-FIVE YEARS

MAY 11, 2018

I've been playing the game of married life for thirty-five years. A review of the Life Tile prize cards in the new version of The Game of Life reveals what I knew all along: I didn't need a gold foil banner declaring 'Same Male Appendage Forever' to make it this far.

I'll go ahead and admit it from the get go: I am a bit of a prude. The realization hit me after seeing — for probably the tenth time — a bridal shower banner on Instagram proudly declaring: 'SAME PENIS FOREVER'. The words made me cringe a little.

Even so, I was curious and Googled the banner and clicked on the Amazon site link (because they are the biggest, so obviously their banner would be the best), and discovered the banner is in stock. Unfortunately, beneath that in red it stated 'This item does not ship to your selected location.'

That earned a momentary *WTF*?

But then, I understood the problem.

Given that whatever I search for on Amazon shows up as an advertisement within five minutes on the next website I hop on to, a reminder that I really, really need this new thing — I am aware that Amazon is all-knowing about my life. It will not ship a 'SAME PENIS FOREVER' gold foil banner to my home for one reason and one reason only. I have been playing the game of married life for thirty-five years.

Quite clearly, Amazon doesn't think I need to buy a gold foil reminder.

I haven't been playing the game alone. Dr. K has helped out. But when we were in the process of becoming a married couple back in 1983, there weren't any penis banners available for purchase on the internet. I hate to date myself so drastically, but there wasn't an internet either.

You can relax. There was one of 'those' bakeries that baked 'those' kinds of cakes (the pink ones, that were, um, shaped in the shape of a, um, male appendage, aka, penis). So maybe we sort of knew what we were getting ourselves into on that torrentially rainy day on the last Saturday in May 1983.

And yet, here I sit typing and wondering whether I missed out on a gold foil guarantee that my marriage would last. If I'd had the gold foil penis banner, I could have placed it in the box with my wedding dress — if I could remember where that box was. But more importantly, if I had a gold foil penis banner, would that make my life more complete?

In the spirit of self-evaluation, I pulled out the box containing The Game of Life. And discovered it wasn't the same Game of Life I remembered when I was a kid. Somehow, we'd acquired the new Millennial version.

That happens a lot at our house. These boxes imprinted with the Mona Lisa Amazon smile mysteriously show up on a near daily basis. I suspect it has something to do with Dr. K's trigger-finger order affliction.

This new version of The Game of Life is much more interesting than the 1960s version I grew up with. That one focused on the number of children you would birth, whether you had life insurance, a college education, and could safely land in Millionaire Acres for the Golden Years. These days, players also receive awards for what one of my acquaintances terms 'do-goodery' — basically like recycling trash and helping the homeless. There are a lot more life activities that are possible in the Millennial version. Inflation had blown up the prize money, too.

So I took stock of the last thirty-five years.

1. Adopt a pet (no monetary allotment)**:** This was one of the cards players could draw, instead of the special Life Tiles with achievements and corresponding prize money. Adopting pets doesn't pay out prize money, but we have learned through adoption of one mutt named Molly, the purchase of four collies (in batches of two), and an array of short-lived cats, how pet ownership comes with a guaranteed payout for years in vet bills. We've also vicariously added a hedgehog (daughter's) and a Shiba Inu (son and daughter-in-law's) into the family, but don't have to pay for them. There is something to be said for grand-pets.

2. Save Endangered Species ($200,000): The United States Fish & Wildlife Service has five criteria for designation as an endangered species. Between our two kids, they accumulated enough experiences to earn them both that designation. Although we were accustomed to wild animals living in our home, the two human animals I'd birthed turned out to be more challenging than all the four-footed ones listed above, combined. The criteria were met, as follows:

- *The present or threatened destruction, modification, or curtailment of its habitat or range:*
  - After local police squad cars with flashing cherry lights showed up in our driveway at midnight when my son was hosting a party, his car keys were confiscated, thereby modifying and curtailing his habitat.
- *Over-utilization for commercial, recreational, scientific, or educational purposes:*
  - Certainly, payment and support of both kids' pursuit of education for a combined thirty-seven years and counting meets this criteria point.
- *Disease or predation:*
  - Wouldn't you think that when your daughter earns the title, 'Lemon Jello Shot Queen', thanks to her supplying a party with aforementioned lemon Jello shots, it is a sign of disease or predation?
- *The inadequacy of existing regulatory mechanisms:*
  - When planning for a family, we thought two children were an ideal number for two parents. Offering a 1:1 ratio, it

seemed that the elements of control and oversight were in place. But then there were those senior proms that went awry. It's called, "being outnumbered by teenagers with raging hormones."

- *Other natural or manmade factors affecting its survival:*
  - A tally of visits to the ER due to jumping off roofs, ski accidents, pole vaulting mishaps, bicycling miscalculations, tennis and running injuries, and driving our cars (carelessly) adds up to a lengthy list of factors which threatened their survival.

The human animals we'd allowed to live were saved by the beneficial aspects of time. It washes away memories, dulls pain, dilutes embarrassment, and adds a glimmer of humor to whatever seemed so damned awful at the time.

3. Discover New Planet ($100,000): We've been trying to find a new planet, but despite twelve moves, purchasing (and remodeling) five houses, and making cross country treks to kids in college and grad school, it is as yet undiscovered. However, I believe the aforementioned activity should count towards those efforts.

4. Become President ($250,000): It doesn't say 'become president' of what. Dr. K and I have managed to be elected to the presidency of too many non-profit organizations to count, all of which was volunteer time. Therefore, I think the prize money is due. We'll happily deposit it in our joint bank account, but I get to spend three quarters of the proceeds because my tally of volunteer hours is three quarters more than his.

5. Design New Computer ($100,000): An acknowledgment of failure here — Dr. K does have a mistress — her name is Apple. Over the years, he has rebuilt dozens of computers, one of which was the Blueberry-flavored iMac G3 which he attempted to turn into an aquarium. It either leaked or the fish died, I can't remember which, but it wasn't a moneymaker. I think at least three times the prize money is due from Apple as compensation for discovering that their computers leak.

6. Write Great American Novel ($150,000): I've written two novels, and a handful of people think they're really great, so does that count?

7. Pulitzer Prize ($100,000): This has not happened yet, but with the third novel in the works — at least in my head — and a children's picture book collaboration with my daughter-in-law, I'm not giving up hope yet.

8. Cure the Common Cold ($200,000): Ever since graduating from medical school in 1987, Dr K keeps trying to cure people. Along the way the old adage to feed people chicken soup has crept into his skills. He doesn't actually cook the soup, but is great at dismembering and grilling chickens. This includes exploratory ventures into spatchcocking, a rotisserie, and chicken sous vide. Carcasses are carefully stored in the freezer in ziplock baggies so 'someone' can make chicken soup.

9. Find New Energy Source ($200,000): Don't ever let anyone tell you that naps are overrated.

10. Invent New Sport ($50,000): Juggling work, children, five people's schedules, dogs with epilepsy, and extended family while walking forward with your eyes closed. Oh — wait, that sport has already been invented. It's called The Game of Life.

I returned to the Amazon site and once more pondered purchasing the gold foil penis banner. After spending all this time taking stock, I think I'm much too tired to hit the 'order now' button. I think I'll take a nap instead.

WHEN AMERICAN APPLE PIE MET THE MELTING POT

JUNE 8, 2018

During a five-day stint in NYC, I realized Americans still love apple pie, but our icons today reflect multicultural influences. Here are a few to consider.

The other day at the grocery store, I picked up a copy of the *Farmers' Almanac* and idly leafed through its pages while waiting to check out.

Yes, it was that *Farmers' Almanac*, still in print since 1818, the one full of planting advice, full moon schedules, and how to prevent tomato hornworms in summer. Luckily, those images of the spiky creatures were photographed in black and white.

But another photo caught my eye — striking even in its monochromic simplicity — one of a young, blonde girl waving an American flag. It prefaced a story about American icons we identify with culturally, an amalgamation of Americana similar to the sorts of things you might happen upon at an estate sale.

The *Farmers' Almanac* story defined America in terms of nostalgic icons: the American bald eagle, white picket fences, Thanksgiving, Norman Rockwell, the little red wagon, and Uncle Sam. All have different levels of significance. Some, like the bald eagle and Thanksgiving, are legislated; others, like Uncle Sam, are the stuff of legend and possibly myth.

But after a recent visit to New York City for my son's medical school graduation, I sense there are other, equally iconic symbols representing what defines America today.

Balto: While the bald eagle is our national bird, as a bird of prey, it's not a friendly species. It thrives on opportunism and feeding off the little guy. I prefer Balto, a Siberian husky who led a team of sled dogs from Nenana to Nome, Alaska in 1925 to deliver diphtheria antitoxin to people dying from the epidemic. Frigid winter weather conditions, ice, and snow made it impossible for planes to fly from Anchorage to Nome, hence the reason the 650 mile trek across the Iditarod trail was undertaken in a relay run by 20 teams of dogsleds to deliver the serum. Balto's driver was a Norwegian named Gunnar Kaasen.

The team's epic journey is memorialized by a statue of Balto in Central Park. At the base of the statue there is the inscription 'Endurance. Fidelity. Intelligence.'

A visit to Balto in Central Park serves as a reminder of what can be achieved on behalf of others in spite of brutal conditions.

Skyscrapers: While the white picket fence may still enclose the dream home for some Americans, others are equally happy living in a tower that touches the sky. It's a different sort of communal living, with shared common spaces and no grass to mow. And the picket fence doesn't need a fresh coat of paint every few years.

Ramen noodle shops: I enjoy Thanksgiving as an opportunity for perfecting my gravy-making skills and its notoriety as a one-day food coma. It's a feast that the almanac says is centered on faith.

But in NYC, you can celebrate life with ramen noodles on a daily basis. Bowls of ramen noodles are available 24/7. Equally a family meal, there is nothing like slurping noodle soup with your loved ones. Did you know that slurping is considered a compliment in Asian countries? The noodle is celebrated by many different cultures: the Italians, Chinese, Koreans, and Japanese are only a few. There is even a religion, Pastafarianism, with its own deity, the Flying Spaghetti Monster. You can give thanks for noodles on every block of NYC.

Subway art: While Norman Rockwell's paintings provide a window into a world of idyllic microcosms, those Camelotian visions are gilded by a halo glow. I prefer looking up when I'm going down, and one of the best spots to do that is the mosaic tile mural, *Funktional Vibrations,* an artwork by Xenobia Bailey in the entrance hall of the 34th Street – Hudson Yards subway station.

The work, which addresses 'the universal idea of creation' is drawn from Bailey's African-American traditions and music of the Sixties. It's definitely got a psychedelic vibe going that will either send your senses swirling or put you into an upbeat frame of mind. I like to think of it as art on acid.

Bicycle delivery services: Maybe the iconic Little Red Wagon holds a special place in Americans' hearts, but design-wise, it's full of flaws. The low profile makes it easy for the rider to fall out of the vehicle whenever a radical turn is taken around a corner, its metal body is prone to rusting, and worst of all, someone has to pull it for you to get any forward motion.

That's why I believe the bicycle — and the bicycle delivery guys, specifically — should be the new American icon. On a bicycle, the navigational abilities of expert riders allow them to dodge NYC traffic, which qualifies as miraculous. And the fact that dinner can be obtained without hazarding the streets of New York make these intrepid cyclists near saints.

Horace Greeley: My hometown, Greeley, Colorado, exists thanks to the backing of New-York Tribune editor Horace Greeley, who encouraged Nathan Meeker to 'Go West, young man!' and develop a community based on Utopian ideals. Greeley was an advocate of abolition, civil rights, political reform, and ran a failed presidential campaign in 1872.

I was charmed when happening upon Horace Greeley Square at the intersection of Broadway, Avenue of the Americas, and West 32nd Street. It was nice to see a familiar face and name in the middle of the metropolises' throngs.

What impressed me most was the gathering of multicultural young people enjoying lunch and sunshine at the base of the reformer's statue. As we walked through the heart of Koreatown in search of what Yelp promised was 'the best ramen shop ever', it struck me that Greeley was successful after all.

As we draw near to the Fourth of July and celebrations of the founding of our country, I thought it worthwhile to share a few of our most populous city's icons. It prompted considerations of who we are as Americans today, where we are headed, and what we might leave behind in the mists of nostalgia.

CAPTURING CROATIAN *FJAKA* FROM A BICYCLE SEAT

NOVEMBER 2, 2018

Fjaka is peace of mind, taking a break from responsibilities, making an unusual connection, discovering the different.

The first day of a bicycle tour always features a litmus test tricked out as a short excursion. Less an opportunity to shake out travel jitters, it's more a chance for tour leaders to get a read on the group's makeup. Who are the leisurely bikers, who doesn't remember to signal when turning, who will be miles ahead of the group — all can be determined during that brief ride.

I was recovering from a cold that had settled into my lungs. I hoped that first day's short ride in Croatia would give me a recovery day before the real climbing began.

Because we were in Croatia, specifically Brač and Hvar, two of the Dalmatian islands, to hill-climb. That was why Dr. K had chosen this particular destination for a week of active travel.

The string of 79 islands in the Adriatic are relatively low altitude if you're coming from Colorado. Even so, the strikingly beautiful hills, or 'Croatian undulations', as my friend Diane christened them, are relentless.

Not one to wile away hours on a beach, Dr. K said we could marvel at their beauty while perched on the seat of a bicycle. I had expected an exhausting week biking in Croatia.

That first ride on the narrow road up to Dol on the Island of Brač included its own set of 'undulations', a total of six and a half miles. Already there were more hills than first day rides of past trips we had taken.

So it seemed contradictory when Neven, one of our group leaders, introduced me to the Croatian concept of *fjaka* later that evening.

"*Fjaka* is Croatia's way of taking a siesta, except we can do it anytime we want to," Neven explained.

"Like zoning out?" I asked.

The minibus we were riding in shuddered, gathering its gears for another upward lurch. The bus groaned and rounded yet another switchback. We were returning to Dol, the destination for that night's welcome dinner. I looked out the window into the darkening countryside, lulled by the thought that this was one hill we didn't have to climb again. Check that one off the list.

"You will see," he said.

Neven, ship captain, seasoned cyclist, man of few words, didn't explain further.

But I wondered. There was the daily schedule of miles to log cycling, crammed with roadside stops to see olive oil museums, quaint villages, and stone churches. There was one of the world's oldest stonecutting schools to tour in Pučisča, particularly interesting since Brač limestone is incorporated into the White House's architecture. On a more commonplace level, there were meals to consume and nineteen strangers riding with us to become acquainted with.

And with an 8:30 am (sharp) assembly for group instructions each morning, where were we to wedge in this siesta-*fjaka*?

I began to see that night at dinner how *fjaka* defines the Croatian way of thinking.

As the group spilled out of the bus, Marco, the evening's host, welcomed us to his family's castle, a stone villa dating to the fifteenth century. It had been in his family since 1739.

To break the ice, the evening began on the terrace with grappa sipping (walnut, black olive, and an herbal infusion), followed by peka, a meat stew made from lamb, veal, chicken, potatoes, and vegetables sharing a lidded iron pot cooked over an open fire. The dish takes hours to prepare, simmering as the flavors blend, each ingredient contributing the best of itself. The broth is simple and sustaining.

Croatian cuisine pulls from family recipes hundreds of years old, from neighboring Austria, Hungary, Slovenia, Italy, and Croatia –

formerly Yugoslavia. The recipes reflect the country's turbulent history, a testament to its many occupiers and conquerors.

After dinner, Marco invited us to visit the upper level of his home. He led us into a dining room with hand-painted walls of peeling Art Nouveau grandeur, graced by an ornate chandelier where intertwined lilies danced, lending their elongated forms to support the electric bulbs.

The chandelier's flickering light illuminated his ancestors' faces in portraits hung along the walls. On the table lay more faces. Books of family history, photo albums, all were open for us strangers to thumb through. In them, I began to see that *fjaka* is about making unexpected connections.

In front of me was a book of medicine, authored by a woman. I opened it and a photograph of a stern woman with a hint of a smile stared back at me from the delicate pages, her glasses owlish and polished, her eyes clear.

"Her name was Jenny," Marco explained. "She was my grandmother. She trained in Dresden, Germany to become a doctor and she wrote this book on the practice of medicine."

I mentioned that my grandmother had trained to be a physician in Vienna during the same period.

Here, thousands of miles from Colorado, a faded book in a Croatian village had created an unlikely connection. Here there were two grandmothers who had learned the art of medicine in European universities at a time when only a handful of women were doctors. And here in this room were the progeny of two of them.

"Most of what was written 100 years ago about the care and upkeep of the human body is now irrelevant with new scientific discoveries improving diagnoses and treatment methodology," Marco said. "But anatomy, that's still 100 percent accurate. Human physiology hasn't changed."

For the rest of that week cycling the Dalmatian hills, we tested the limits of human physiology while absorbing a new culture.

Beth, one of the group who was soon to move from stranger to definable, likable person, had visited the medical center in Split earlier that first day. She was concerned that her blurred vision might be something more significant than a smear of sunscreen in her eye. For 460 kuna (a whopping $60), she was given a hall pass to ride for the week, armed with the understanding that with age, our bodies relax and connections loosen.

As we explored the Croatian landscape, the group encouraged one another to keep climbing.

There were strenuous hill climbs on Brač and Hvar, a knife-edged island with vistas plummeting to the sea, where narrow roads swooped, tracing the landscape.

When oxygen became scarce and my legs were shaky, I experienced *fjaka* when I stopped trying to process what I saw.

The memory of the face from the pages of the old medical text returned often.

I saw it while pedaling through Stari Grad Plain, an agricultural landscape systemically divided by ancient stone walls, land that has been tilled since Ionian Greeks in the fourth century B.C.

I pondered the complicated history of Croatia while standing on the rain-washed balcony of our hotel room in Postira, watching clouds make impressionist paintings on the water's surface in the harbor.

And as I listened to the cadence of laughter while new friends splashed in the waters of the Adriatic during a refreshing break off the saddles, I took a step back from life.

Even while pedaling, there were pockets of *fjaka*.

It happened after a drenching ride downhill in the rain, when we wrung out our wet outerwear and shared a pizza. And *fjaka* happened after making the decision to skip the afternoon ride — without guilt.

It happened drifting off to sleep listening to laughter and raucous song from the *konoba* across the harbor in Postira, and it happened when, awakened at four in the morning by silence, I rose to consider the harbor lights pooling on the water and then returned to bed.

Fjaka was drinking a beer at eleven in the morning at a *konoba* in Stari Grad, a village dating to the fourth century B.C., knowing it was time for coffee, and not caring.

Fjaka is peace of mind, taking a break from responsibilities, making an unusual connection, discovering the different.

It is also noticing clouds — and not posting the moment on Instagram because it takes too much effort to find your smartphone.

It is the realization that the world isn't as big as we think it is and people are much the same.

On the cramped trip home, sipping a Bloody Mary in a real glass which the flight attendant gave me for reasons unfathomable, I sat and watched the screen on the back of the seat where a simulation of our plane inched its way west across the Atlantic.

And I realized, *fjaka* isn't something you do. It's what you make time for in your life every day.

And sometimes, it happens without even thinking about it.

ATLANTA UNDERGROUND

JANUARY 1, 2019

From Oakland Cemetery to Clermont Lounge, Atlanta is a city obsessed with its history, much of which lies underground.

Atlanta is a city obsessed with what lies below its surface. From the currently defunct but to-be-resurrected Underground Atlanta shopping and dining arcade, to the revered Oakland Cemetery, beneath the bumpy sod of which slumber Atlanta's famed citizens without regard to the all-too-lively goings-on above them, the city's streets also reverberate from the happenings below ground.

It's partly thanks to the ladies who dance at the fabled Clermont Lounge in the basement of the Hotel Clermont.

We first visited the city nearly twenty-five years ago. At the time, it was a community I believed should be solely dedicated to Scarlett O'Hara — because wasn't it she and Ashley Wilkes and that lumber mill who helped rebuild Atlanta after the Confederate Army and Sherman burned it to the ground in 1864? Wait, you may say: that was only a story.

Gone with the Wind isn't real, Emily, you might say.

It was real enough for Margaret Mitchell, whose gravestone we visited at Oakland, who once said she used to think *Gone with the Wind* was her book, but her thinking had changed — it was Atlanta's book, Atlanta's story.

That first time I visited Atlanta, I searched in vain to find Margaret Mitchell's and Scarlett's Atlanta. On my recent visit, I believe I uncovered it.

The first visit, we were in the city for a medical conference. That meant Dr. K went off to meetings and I played the good wife and dallied around museums to amuse myself during the day. At night, we would reconvene for dinner.

On that visit twenty-five years ago, the hotel concierge directed us to a southern barbecue joint in Underground Atlanta, a shopping and entertainment district built in 1969 in Five Points. I enthusiastically endorsed the concierge's suggestion. Five Points was a name sounding remotely familiar, culled from the book that had become my bible for all things Georgia.

As with many shopping centers constructed in that era, Underground Atlanta had become decrepit, often the scene of drug deals, hold ups at gunpoint, and seedy dining establishments with stringy meat disguised as food that was only edible after generous applications of mustardy BBQ sauce. Murders were not uncommon along the shopping corridors. There was one reported on the front page of the Atlanta Journal-Constitution the morning after our uneasy barbecue excursion.

But a city can change in twenty-five years. And Atlanta has transformed, in many ways for the better. Warehouses and industrial buildings have been repurposed, filled with foodie hotspots and unique boutiques. It has become a vibrant city, welcoming a multicultural population with easily accessible ethnic experiences.

But the people of Atlanta continue to hang on to the past in unfathomable ways.

We stayed at the Hotel Clermont by a fluke. It happened to be the hotel nearest Harrison's and Alex's apartment; they had recently moved to the city for Harrison's residency years. The hotel had been renovated to the tune of $30 million and only reopened last July. TripAdvisor reviews were flattering, underscoring the hotel's hipster vibe. Not much was said about its famed dancing ladies.

The hotel website played up its quirkiness. In understated hues of Flamingo Pink and Vespa Peppermint Green, with a typewriter font and pen-and-ink drawings depicting good times in pajamas, the message was playful, inviting, and reminiscent of one of my favorite movies, *Victor, Victoria*. What could the harm be? And it was only a ten-minute walk to the kids' place. In a town of five million, that's worth a second look.

There were hints in the reviews about noise from the lounge. Having stayed in many hotels over the years, I know you're playing

Russian Roulette with the chance that you'll be placed in a room for six nights next to an elevator that rattles, no matter how swanky the hotel and the island. Elevators are machines. They're not perfect.

The Hotel Clermont was starting off business with an open playbook, noting the potential for sleep disruptions. But we realized they might be serious about it when we pulled open the drawers of the bedside tables and found earplugs and a card offering soothing white noise machines, available at the front desk.

You know, those bright orange earplugs you roll between your fingers and then massage into your ears before taking off on a flight. The ones people wear when operating loud machines in case there might be damage to your hearing.

At first, I considered it a minor price to pay for the beautifully decorated, bandbox-fresh Art Deco hotel room. With a cozy corner of windows outfitted with a chaise lounge, it was the perfect spot to wile away the hours reading — or to contemplate the world after a busy holiday season.

But I learned from the card on the bedside table that the Lounge — the famous Clermont Lounge filled with ladies dancing beneath Atlanta's streets — opened at one in the afternoon and the action kept going until three in the morning. The dancers took Sundays off. The music began subtly around three o'clock or so, just when you were considering that a rainy afternoon nap sounded lovely before changing to head to dinner. The crescendo increased, reaching full throttle around 11 pm, with the booming (and accompanying grinding and grating) coming to a halt at 3 am, on the dot.

You have to understand that the Clermont Lounge is an Atlanta icon, if not a gem.

In operation since 1965, the Clermont Lounge is Atlanta's first and longest operating strip club. The dancers, typically of baby boomer-era birth, have bodies representative of real women, heavy on the fleshy attributes. The current star, since 1978, is Blondie, a dancer famous for her ability to crush empty Budweiser and PBR cans between her prodigious breasts. Before that was Tiny Lou, who is commemorated in the name of the Hotel Clermont's swanky restaurant, a high-end nod to French cuisine. The hotel itself has been open in numerous iterations since 1924, when it was christened the Clermont Motor Hotel. When Fulton County health inspectors finally closed the hotel on December 31, 2009 — dirty linen and bed bugs were only the beginning of the problems — a one-bedroom apartment rented for $185 a week.

These days, the going rate for a room at the gentrified hotel is, on average, $269 a night. I'm not good at math, but it seems like gentrification has its benefits for the gentrifiers.

The dancers below the streets, beneath the Hotel Clermont, are not going anywhere. As with the dead lying quietly in Oakland Cemetery beneath church-like mausoleums, they are revered, if not for their lifestyle, then for their history.

It doesn't matter much to the front desk that after two nights at the hotel I dreaded going to sleep. On the last night of our six-night stay, we finally begged them to switch us to a quieter room.

But my sleep deprivation isn't the story.

The strippers at the Clermont Lounge have a right to earn a living. In many cases, it's the only way these women can support their families. I have a friend in Denver who lives next door to a houseful of women strippers. They are women with children, they go to teacher conferences, they scramble for a healthy dinner to feed their offspring. For many, it isn't a profession of choice, but it is a profession that pays the grocery bill.

And Atlanta gets that. It is a city that exists above and below the ground. It is a city with a cemetery boasting monuments of near church-like stature, a cemetery where you can be married on its grounds, standing on the coffins of your ancestors.

It is also a city reflective of the needs of all its peoples.

Margaret Mitchell understood that. In addition to writing about the conflict between the North and the South, she wrote about the tension between two women — Scarlett O'Hara, and her nemesis, Belle Watling — the whorehouse madam who was equally loved by Rhett Butler, who likely bore him a son. The Clermont Lounge didn't exist when Mitchell penned her classic book. But even so, there is a thread of the story that continues, epitomized by the women of Atlanta today who live most of their lives underground.

YES, MR. NOVELIST.
I AM A FOOD WRITER

FEBRUARY 8, 2019

Whether writing about food or novels, someone will criticize your efforts. And most often, I am the first in line to sign up and criticize myself.

A couple years ago, I crawled out of bed on a Saturday morning at an ungodly hour and drove south for miles on end to attend a conference for writers. I label it ungodly because, as a night owl, anything earlier than dawn breaking — plus a couple hours under its belt to see how the day is going to pan out — deserves that adjective.

The town we live in is bordered on four sides by agriculture. As such, it's a town surrounded by those who celebrate a rooster's existence. But as a town girl residing inside those agricultural borders, if there are roosters crowing, I can't hear them.

I don't fault the rooster. Thanks to eons of repetition and the activity's proven success in yanking people within earshot out of bed, the rooster has earned his right to crow at the sun.

However, for someone who finds it impossible to drift off before the moon has risen, and before my brain's gyrations have been subdued by vodka and dinner, the bird of the morning is irrelevant. Even though we could raise chickens in town, and in spite of Dr. K's frequent pestering to get some, there are no roosters or other loud feathered friends in our backyard.

But back to this writers' conference. Networking conferences can be self-defeating, and yet, I spurred myself to wake up and attend.

The conference was heralded as an event guaranteed to improve my literary skills, establish literary credentials, and help align me with people having marketing know-how. The invisible subtext was that it was one of those networking things calculated to wring understanding from your ego that you are an absolutely worthless person, one who should drop any dream of making writing a calling, one who should find some other career to make you happy.

To put this in perspective, as a shoe fanatic, I've often entertained the thought of shoe-selling as a likely career choice. Those of you who find the aroma of a new car or caramel corn aphrodisiacal will identify with how the scent of a thing will make you want to dedicate your life to selling it. The pristine odor of a new shoe rockets my heart skywards. It does the same for my collie, Mopsy, who will do anything she can to stuff her long nose into shoe leather and inhale its delectableness. If it's Italian shoe leather, that much the better.

Before attending this conference, much as Mopsy loves Italian shoe leather, the aroma of a hardcover book sent my senses reeling.

But, back to this event that required several hours of early morning driving. As a writers' conference, it aimed to chat up others working in the industry to teach writers how to sell books. The between-the-lines meaning of these things is that there could be hope of commiseration, or at least mutual agreement that writing books is a miserable existence.

As it happened, the very worst part of the day spent at the writers' conference ended up having nothing to do with the drive. If I had known how conversations would evolve, I would have kept driving.

I was introduced to a fellow writer, one who had won an award for his book from the organization holding the conference. We chatted it up for several minutes — comparing notes from one novelist to another — before he dropped 'the statement'.

This happened because he had discovered I write a blog about recipes and about life.

"You're a food writer," he said.

He delivered this short line with an actual lip curl. You know it. Often mistaken for a facial tic, there is that lip wrinkle on the right side of a person's mouth. Most likely, it's an unconscious motion. The degree of lip movement is slight, and yet, it exists, particularly if you are one of those people like me who make a daily effort to crawl out from beneath your down-filled duvet to face the world and await its criticism.

"Well, yes," I stumbled, "I do write a food blog but I've also written a novel, um, which also won an award like yours did (except mine was national and I figured he could read that if he looked at the sticker on the book's cover), but most of the time I develop recipes and jot down my weird views of the world on my blog."

There was that tic again, which could likely have been Tourette's Syndrome or some other transient tic disorder. I was probably reading him all wrong.

So I went and sat down in my seat and tried to imagine I was anywhere else but here, several hours away from home on a Saturday morning. I ardently wished I were sitting at the kitchen table, reading my city's newspaper, sipping coffee, and ladling salsa over my eggs.

On the drive home I chanted, "You're a food writer," all the way. I chanted it for all the 83.7 miles, in contrapuntal harmony. The chorus went, "And you really ought to be selling shoeeeeees!"

It was a beautiful ending to a symphony of woefulness.

That was 2012. Since then, I've created 284 recipes, and 171 often weird blog posts. I wrote another novel, which people tell me they've enjoyed reading. And yeah, it won an award or two. And somewhere along the line, someone read what I was releasing from my brain hours after the roosters crowed and asked me if I'd like to write stories about food for a newspaper. My newspaper. My city.

I've come to accept that for some, writing about restaurants and food may seem a fluffy enterprise. At times, I have to agree. It's just food on a plate. What does it taste like? It tastes like food.

But observing and writing about what appears on a plate can transport you into many a philosophical conversation. About science, about art, about how we think as humans, about the world itself.

It's a bit like my novels. People ask me what my novels are about.

"Um, they're stories about people. Like a piece of art, a study on a topic, I write people studies," is what I usually say.

I meet the most interesting people every day, and often, they share stories of their life with me. They ask me to write their story, like the man from Vietnam who told me he had seen everything. There was nothing he hadn't seen, he said. And would I write about it?

Food is life, and life is food. We have to respect and admire all the angles, all the possibilities. As a food writer, I also write people studies.

It's a pretty simple concept. Without food, there is no life. How foods have developed over the millennia is pretty damned fascinating. Observing what others create, and then figuring out a way to help people understand the where's and why's of how food is created is larger than the circumference of a dinner plate. There is philosophy, human psychology, mathematics, and even physics.

I want readers to enjoy a meal as much as I do. In enjoying food, I hope people will enjoy life just that little bit more.

Food and its preparation is an art form, no matter how fleeting. So should we feel shame in consuming it, or describing its equally fleeting enjoyment?

CONSIDERING THE STUFF OF DREAMS

MARCH 8, 2019

In our dreams, our minds relax, pulling from a collection of images stored in our brains, sorted and processed, giving meaning, fostering creativity.

I sent an email to a friend several weeks ago at three in the morning. It seemed reasonable enough to me. In fact, it was necessary.

I had been talking with Dr. K for a couple of days about how this friend's husband had undergone surgery on his right arm. Dr. K suggested it would be nice to reach out to her and see how he was doing, particularly since the surgery had spanned two days.

I had been berating myself because I had forgotten to send the email.

"How thoughtless!" I told myself. "You should have sent that email yesterday!"

So I sent it right there and then, at three in the morning from the darkness of my bed. An arm, seemingly disconnected to the rest of me, fumbled for my cell phone to send the note. The disembodied fingers typed the phantom thought while I watched in detached amazement: how did the fingers access the cell phone to begin with?

Of course, it was all a dream.

There had been no surgery for two days. There had been no surgery at all. My friend responded to my query several hours later, her confusion evident. Had I perhaps been thinking of another friend?

I replied that I hadn't. And I said, "Well, that was quite the dream."

In dreams, we can rework the oddest of occurrences, weaving threads of conversation into story.

As a lifelong insomniac, 'insomnia' is a word I don't want to look at, much less think about. The word is an evil totem, one that, if voiced, can curse nights of sleep going forward. Insomnia, the bane of human reason, is defined as the "abnormal inability to get enough sleep." It's a word that can excoriate existence.

There are plenty of warnings about the effects of sleeplessness based on sleep studies, stories of the ills that can afflict the human body when we don't get enough sleep. Decreased tolerance of pain. Inability to focus on work resulting in reduced productivity. In Japan, workers suffer from chronic overwork, with increasing incidences of *karoshi*. This doesn't mean you're heading to your favorite karaoke bar after knocking off work. It means death from working too much. Americans may not be all that far behind.

Simply reading about the human failure to sleep is frightening because we have failed at doing what nature requires.

But as much as I fear the possibility of insomnia, at times my dreams bring their own concerns.

Consider dogs. We are admonished to let a sleeping dog lie.

You know what happens if you touch a sleeping dog? I'm often tempted to do it. They're so cute, lying there. Each of our collies has a bed in the kitchen because that's the place where we live. After spending their day chasing away bunnies, barking at birds who have the nerve to fly over collie territory without requesting security clearance, and maintaining bark patrol over the neighborhood, Flopsy and Mopsy are tired. Relaxed in their slumbers, they have abandoned consciousness. Their paws run, paddling air, in search of that elusive stray sheep. What might happen should they encounter it, carelessly nibbling on the grass of a neighbor's pasture — or the equivalent, today's lawn?

When awake, Mopsy is a relatively pleasant dog. It's true, she barks a lot. But realize, she has an important job to do as neighborhood watchdog.

But when the collies are in this relaxed state of dogdom, that's when I want to stretch out beside them to cuddle. For the most part, they don't seem to mind. But when startled out of a particularly deep sleep, Mopsy tends to jump. She gathers herself, jolted from the pastoral place in which she wanders, transforming into a tense and snarling mass of unfriendly fur, snapping at whoever treads unknowingly across her dreams.

In sleep, our minds relax, telling us that what seems real is in fact just so. Our minds pull from a collection of images stored in our brains; the images are sorted and processed, giving meaning, and fostering creativity.

As an insomniac, I obsessively scroll through topics while trying to fall asleep.

And like Mopsy, the biggest problem I have when trying to channel sleep is my brain. It refuses to shut down — there are pop-up windows indicating that certain programs and applications are stuck. Word processing is particularly demonic, as are photos. They are tied to each other and invariably, as I sort through stories, I have to engage the manual force-quit.

But a most curious thing about your mind is what happens when your brain begins to shut down. At first running in circles, your brain caches data while grasping at meaning. It analyzes, sorts, and categorizes what it knows must be processed before the next step can be taken. It seeks answers to questions you surely should have tackled before preparing dinner — answers which you should have filed away by the time you've consumed two glasses of wine.

In sleep, one might think the human brain is the equal of a dog's. And as you settle into sleep, paws paddling air, your brain is in search of that elusive sheep. On any given night, you may find yourself settling into a close-eyed planning session with a staff of one with intermittent breaks spent in the bathroom, acknowledging how futile it is to seek the glory of sleep. Those nights are when insomnia reigns.

But then, there are those elusive nights when the dream magic happens.

Yes. We've all had that dream of wearing a blue silk taffeta Cinderella dress — just like the one at Chatsworth House, the one where the Queen of Heaven peeps over our shoulder. And we're wearing the dragonfly pin. Of course.

It Starts with a Fish

There are the nights when the words which have failed me by day miraculously writ themselves large across my sleeping brain. They are the nights when impressions, inscrutable in daylight, are illuminated when censorship falls away. Those are the nights when you make movies, write books, and concoct myths.

At times, those are the nights when you send phantom emails to friends who are confused by your abstraction.

And yet, ever in search of creativity, the little missteps are worth it. Even when they occur in dreams.

THE THIRTY PERCENT RULE

APRIL 5, 2019

The thirty percent rule of housing affordability might be said to apply to shopping sales, and living life to its thirty-percent fullest.

I heard a story the other day about an older woman who was driving her car with a set of bald tires. A friend suggested she purchase a new set because she was concerned for her friend's safety on the roads. Instead of buying new tires, the older woman decided to stop driving. When her friend asked her why, she said, "I may not live long enough to wear new ones out."

In a sense, the story reminds me of a gift from my sister of a box of Bertie Bott's Every Flavor Beans. It also reminds me of recent longings for tangerine espadrilles.

For those of you who aren't Harry Potter fans, Bertie Bott's (jelly bean) flavors are a bit off-the-wall. You can equally expect to gum a piña colada bean as one that tastes like vomit. I've tasted both bean flavors, because as it happens, they're nearly the same color.

But the gift of a pristine box of Bertie Bott's Beans seemed too precious to open. The box itself is really cute, a visual paean to carnivals, childhood, and everything else that's good about summer and life experienced under a canvas tent.

The unopened box of beans had been bouncing around in my purse until yesterday morning when a friend was looking for a stick of chewing gum in her own purse. We were playing tennis and her mouth was dry. I offered mints, and finding none while rummaging in my purse, happened upon the beans.

"You must eat them!" my friend cried, after I explained their sentimental purpose. "It's bad luck not to enjoy the gift!"

And so we did. And it seemed that the day took on a bit of gilded edging in so doing.

One jelly bean made me realize how important it is not to put life on hold, for what is life if not an experience?

It's a bit like seasonal marketing. Whenever a new season rolls around, it seems that my inbox swells like a river ready to overflow its banks. While it's true that the worst example of this phenomenon happens the day after Halloween, I'd bet even money that the blush of spring fosters some of the most persistent dogging of shoppers for their dollars.

It's easy to figure out why this happens. Who isn't sick and tired of wearing sweaters, boots, and — much as I love the stick-to-me, make-me-somehow-look-thinner qualities of jeggings — I am so ready for flirty sundresses and sandals. Let me breathe!

And that's where the thirty percent rule comes in.

As a matter of budgeting, the common wisdom is to spend no more than thirty percent of your monthly gross income on housing costs. It's a guideline that's been in effect ever since 1981, when the federal government established standards to avoid cost burdens. But somewhere along the line, it became established wisdom that it was okay to budget thirty percent for your wants, the stuff of which tangerine espadrille dreams are made.

That thirty percent rule of budgeting disposable income allows wants like tangerine espadrilles to be on the bargaining table.

It's uncanny that most sales blasted into your inbox are for that exact thirty percent off. Planned, you say?

Here's how it works.

You receive an email notifying you of a sale. The discount offered is only good for twenty-four hours. Suddenly, it becomes your life's purpose to achieve a score.

"Let's grab the deal!" your groggy brain tells you — this, because the thirty percent offer arrives in your inbox at three in the morning.

Fade to scene of sipping coffee at the breakfast table. A laptop is open at your left elbow. Toast crumbs scatter across the placemat.

While scrolling casually through the sale offerings at breakfast, you make mental notes of 'maybe', 'gotta have it', and 'Ha! I'd never wear that!'

Scene: you have left for work with laptop in tow. Brain has realigned for workday demands.

By lunchtime, your sugar levels have dropped, and you're ready to take another swipe through what are now glimmering opportunities to buy new clothes to accentuate springtime playfulness, all thanks to the endorphin release you have experienced at the thought of shopping.

Unfortunately, work gets the better of you, phone calls disrupt good intentions to burn plastic, and besides, those tangerine espadrilles look very familiar. Didn't you buy them last spring and stuff them into the closet? Your mind takes a step back and reviews the contents of your closet. No! You bought the navy-blue ones last year.

But then it's time to make dinner and collapse into bed. "Oh well," you tell yourself. "Another day, another dollar I didn't spend."

The reality is retailers are on to us. They understand the demands of daily life, they get that we are too busy to buy at the slightest provocation. And that's why, suddenly, that thirty percent discount ad resurfaces in your inbox the next morning. The offer has been extended; the sales levels have not yet been hit. What skin is it off Macy's nose to recycle their sale? You say no, then change your mind to yes. In a wave of espresso-driven euphoria, you place the order, only to receive a message that the item you want might be out of stock.

And you mutter to yourself, "Really? Because that was a whole thirty minutes ago. Are there that many people drooling over the size 8 tangerine espadrilles that they're already sold out?"

Resigned to a fate of no tangerine espadrilles in your life — ever — you close the window. Serious depression sets in, only to find a trigger-finger email in your inbox a few hours later. Renewed and refreshed, that thirty percent is offered to you, because you are a VIP. Now, you're hooked. Now you must have those shoes — albeit in another color. Lime green sounds okay. And thirty percent is good! It's what financial advisors tell us we can spend on our wants, our must-haves, our…

But sometimes, an excess of shopping, buying, adding to the bulk in our lives and the stash in the basement only adds up to more of nothing. The wants don't always translate to the needs.

This isn't a blog post about living a life of minimalism. It isn't a question of when do you buy another pair of espadrilles. This isn't about shopping.

It's about listening to the ticking of life's clock and in the process, determining that thirty percent balance of wants, needs, and meaningless inertia. It's about not forgetting to experience life off the couch along the way. And it's about not forgetting to live.

IT'S NOT A VACATION, IT'S RAGBRAI!

AUGUST 9, 2019

RAGBRAI reminds us that Iowa is not the moon. It's a reminder that we are all Americans together. Rain or shine, potholed country roads or highways smooth as glass. It's pride of community and pride of place.

A couple weeks ago, we took a bike ride across flyover country. And as we cycled through Jefferson County, Iowa, I happened upon a guy on a lime-green bicycle wearing a 'We the People' jersey. The preamble of the United States Constitution was printed on it, interspersed with red, white, and blue.

The American heartland, middle America, or whatever label you apply, is that enormous swath of prairie, cornfield, and undulating hills. We were partaking in an annual tradition begun in 1973 by John Karras and Don Kaul, two *Des Moines Register* journalists who accepted a challenge to bicycle across the state. At the time, it was more a publicity stunt than anything. A handful of folks tagged along, including Clarence Pickard of Indianola, who at the age of eighty-three, met the challenge while riding a women's Schwinn, wearing a pith helmet and sporting woolen long underwear beneath his pants.

Forty-seven years later, it's called RAGBRAI — the Register's Annual Great Bicycle Ride Across Iowa.

In a sense, it's a happening of sorts, or as one person I described it to put it, RAGBRAI is the Burning Man for cyclists.

I like to think of it as Iowa's opportunity to show off, a way to spend the state's annual tourism dollars in one fell swoop, a chance to cram the carbon footprint of 15,000 cyclists into one week.

The route varies yearly, with communities vying for the chance to put their towns on display. Each one has a pet fundraiser or several, from grandstands to church furnaces to children's after-school programs. Each one is worthy.

But lest you think RAGBRAI is a sort of joyride, think again. RAGBRAI is a test of stamina, a pedal — in our case — of 462 miles, from Council Bluffs to Keokuk. You dip your rear tire in the Missouri River, your front tire in the Mississippi seven days later.

As with most things, there is a process.

First, you are accepted to ride. You and 8,500 of your soon-to-become closest friends. This translates to thousands of humans cluttering the roadways while perched on self-propelled, easy-to-topple vehicles, one that with each swerve to the left or right comes the possibility that it will be your last swerve on Earth.

We received our letter on May 1st. It was a bit like when Harry Potter received his letter by owl informing him he'd been accepted to Hogwarts School of Witchcraft and Wizardry, only multiplied by 8,500. That's the number of registered riders; on most days the ride swells to well over 15,000. Not all who ride are registered.

Dr. K and I looked at each other with excitement when we received our letters. "We get to ride RAGBRAI," we said in unison.

And then reality hit. "We have to get ready to ride RAGBRAI."

The organizers recommended training, but amounts varied. One source suggested logging 500 miles before dipping your rear tire in the starting river; others cautioned no less than 1,000. We came in a hair above the first and miles below the second.

"It's an adventure," we repeated to ourselves. "It'll build character."

Along with logging miles, we began collecting things. We were going to be in the middle of the Iowan wilds!

As with most adventurers, we felt a kinship with Meriwether Lewis as he checked off equipment to forge a path from St. Louis to the West coast. Amazon boxes began arriving daily. Camping gear, rain gear, all manner of bicycle necessities, and most necessary of all, disposable paper seat covers for the ever-essential KYBO, flyover terminology for port-a-potty.

After surviving the first night in Council Bluffs in a city of over 300 tents, deluged by rain, and scared shitless by lightning, we awoke on day one to a continuing torrential downpour and clambered on our bikes.

"At least the lightning stopped," our group of four acknowledged nervously.

Throughout that week, we pedaled alongside every sort of wheeled conveyance: there were skaters on boards, skaters on skates, recumbent bikes and those powered by hand. There were cyclists pulling trailers with children, with boom boxes, with coolers full of ice. Two-wheelers, tandems, and tricycles — the strongest of strongmen rode a CrossFit machine on wheels. We cheered the Pride of the United States Air Force, with a team of the fittest of the fit, and we complimented Clan Lindsay, dressed in a wide swath of wool tartan.

Halfway through the week, in a little hamlet I can't recall the name of, on a sign in front of a business that is only a blur, the letters read, 'EAT. DRINK. SLEEP. BIKE. REPEAT.'

RAGBRAI is like the movie *Groundhog Day*, except instead of a charming hotel you sleep on an air mattress in a tent, one with sheets that wick up dewy ground moisture like a sponge. After a day of riding through Iowa's humid summer, you find yourself shivering at 3 am, with damp sheets and a groggy awareness that the alarm will go off in a couple of hours so you can get up and do it again.

And if you think about getting back on that bicycle, you think you surely can't. And yet, you straddle it and your brain takes over the legs. There is a certainty of rollers, of humidity and heat, and the guarantee of another hill.

But at every town, the red carpet is unrolled. There are the shy and polite Amish dotting the roadside, selling juicy peaches fresh-picked from their orchards, churning out homemade ice cream with maple syrup, perfect for dolloping on a slice of apple pie. Their pride is quiet, yet no different from that of the sixteen-year-old waitress who served us dinner in Indianola's town square cafe.

Each town is much like the next, the larger ones hosting midday food trucks that follow the bikers no less than cooks followed Napoleon's army. There were evening revelries around courthouses of unlikely grandeur in this land of rustic barns, waving cornfields, and ever-present hog farms. This is the Iowa we saw, hogs and corn, bicycles and blue sky.

"You're in the middle of Iowa, not the moon," the RAGBRAI literature advised.

And Iowa, in its annual weeklong celebration of Iowa, celebrates more than simply itself.

It was a week where petty politics, grievances, and Twittering were shut off. With 15,000 cyclists, support vehicles, and curious throngs on hand to watch the spectacle, the internet was a morass of dead space. It was a week spent in search of morning breakfast bowls overflowing with scrambled eggs, sausage, and cheese, then succumbing to necessity, standing in line at the KYBO before clambering back on the bicycle. It was a week of showering in eighteen-wheelers, the water all too hot, the towels all too skimpy.

We talked with fellow cyclists about how much farther it was until the next killer hill would arise in the distance, and how long we could stress our legs until the next break. Caution and care became part of the herd mentality, and if you happened to leave a roll of cash in a KYBO, the next user was certain to dash out to find you and hand it back.

Thousands of bicycles and not a lock to be seen. On RAGBRAI, you don't worry about theft. You worry about spotting the next pothole so it doesn't kill you.

RAGBRAI is sunshine, cantaloupe ice cream, and the promise of Mr. Porkchop's pink school bus only six miles away. It's pie in the afternoon and Bloody Marys at seven in the morning; it's beer all day, should you want it. It's pickle juice and slices of watermelon wider than a grin. It's a nonstop party, even in the rain. But it's also the hamlet of Walnut, crisscrossed with antique shops from wherever you look.

'Flyover country'. It's a term coined by writer Thomas McGuane in a 1980s' article for *Esquire*.

He came to the phrase after expressing his frustration with the realities of air travel.

'I recall being annoyed that the places I loved in America were places that air travel allowed you to avoid.'

The ride is a reminder that Iowa is not the moon. It's a worthy reminder that we are all Americans together. Rain or shine, with potholed country roads or highways smooth as glass. There is pride of community and pride of place.

It's an opportunity to see a part of our country at a snail's pace. Unless you're zooming downhill.

THANKS TO HINDSIGHT'S 2020, YOU CAN TEACH AN OLD DOG NEW TRICKS

DECEMBER 27, 2019

Hindsight happens when you allow yourself to look back at previous actions to find clarity, process grief, and engage in self-care. And then, begin healing.

A few nights ago, I happened to catch the moon rise at two-thirty in the morning. Marbled and orange, it hugged the horizon, its color borrowed from Earth's raw essence. I could call it fortuitous that I happened to see it, but in truth, I was up then, grasping at a trail of thoughts, hoping to capture them on my cell phone before they drifted back into the ether. It's the writer's curse. The minute your mind relaxes, the ideas burble up and flow out.

It was also late that night when I had another 'aha' moment, when I realized the swirl of chatter about the Roaring Twenties was contemporary, a reference to the decade rolling over before our eyes, and anticipation of the new decade just ahead. Sometimes, when we are too focused on the minutiae, we don't see the point right in front of us. We are blind to what really matters.

Ideas which come to me at night could be called unconscious thought, but I think the better label is hindsight.

And because of my love of words and the search for deeper meaning, e.g. 'feeding the famished', I tend to become entangled in the wrappings of metaphor.

In so doing, I often avoid writing about the truth in some of its ugliest terms. Let's put it this way: Beneath the base of a tree is the root structure supporting it. We might think that the greater the weaving of the intricacies, the stronger the tree. But we need to consider the tree as a whole in order to fully understand it.

With the help of hindsight's 2020, I am forcing myself to look back over the past years.

It has to begin with the year 2019, because it's been incredibly difficult, likely the worst year I've ever had.

I have been buoyed up by the strength of a fellow author who wrote of her losses this year to write the truth of my life as it stands today, even if it hurts to share it.

Back in April, I lost a position with an organization that I've dedicated myself to for over twenty-five years. Although it was a volunteer position, the intent and method with which the company and its board treated me nearly ripped out my soul, leaving me with a bleak question of whether humanity had fallen off course in its quest for self-aggrandizement.

And then, in September, my darling daughter Isabelle succumbed to her bipolar demons, falling down the rabbit hole chasing after them. Currently homeless, she is as unreachable as was Odysseus on his journey. Like Alice, she has likely 'stumbled into a bizarre and disoriented alternate reality.' My greatest wish is that someday Isabelle resurfaces in our lives. Confused, perhaps, but generally intact, ready to pursue a path of healing.

2019 has been bordered by grief, for what was lost, for what might have been. In that, I've experienced a sort of bereavement, torn against my will from an organization I loved and cared about. And light-years worse has been the grieving process for my daughter. The aspirations shattered by her diagnosis and its subsequent unraveling are equal to the ether of my thoughts when I cannot harness them.

Fortunately, my collie Mopsy has been able to show me that you can teach an old dog new tricks.

Mopsy, who is going on eleven, has the tenacious drive and determination of the runt she is. In spite of her birth order, wiry and feisty, she is the alpha of our pack. Mopsy can make her sister Flopsy cower with a steady look in the eye. She can also entice Flopsy out of her comfortably plump lethargy. With a low growl followed by a well-calculated heel nip, the aging dogs become a blur of fangs, claws, and ruffling fur as they chase each other round and round the kitchen, down the hall, and back again.

Where Mopsy excels, though, is innovative thought.

She has a yen for Kleenex, the more used, the better. Since I know this and — when I remember — place tissues out of reach, Mopsy has taken to knocking over the toilet paper stand in our guest bathroom and pulling the (clean) rolls off the chrome arm. After yanking off a couple, she settles in for a nice chew.

It gives me hope that Mopsy, who's creeping up on seventy-seven years this March, has found a new path to make her life more pleasant. For Mopsy, that means it's easier to get what she wants.

She is helping me see how I can take what's important to me — writing and the people who matter to me — and use that to find clarity. I follow her lead, seeking innovation and living with a purpose.

In that vein of seeking clarity and meaning to life, I've always encouraged my daughter Isabelle to search for ladybugs, at least five a day. Ladybugs are our metaphor for randomness that can be viewed positively.

I hope she is putting our ladybug system to good use, wherever she may be.

But I've also realized I need to search for my own ladybugs. They are the harbingers of hindsight. Here are my first steps:

- I can only control my actions.
- I'm going to stop shouldering the blame for the actions of others. They are who they are; their actions are theirs to claim.
- The best action is reaction, and I am in control of that.
- If I drain myself, I will have nothing left to give anyone.
- It's essential to focus less on giving to others who don't want what I can give them, and more on time spent searching for the universal story, one that crystalizes who I am. Who we are.

I'm not sad to see 2019 go. Some years are like that. I am anticipating the Roaring Twenties with great curiosity and some trepidation. Everything in life has its inherent challenges.

I'm not saying there will be less of me that gives, that the nurturing of others will end. But like Mopsy, I plan to live stronger and stop hiding the truth of myself behind what I think people will accept, behind words I hope won't make people cringe.

Life is an unknowable journey, but it's better to take it than not. And while pursuing life, it's okay to give some of it back to yourself.

THE COMMUNITY TANK: A BETTA FISH STORY

FEBRUARY 14, 2020

Although I regularly fall in love with animals of all sorts, betta fish didn't lure me in. Until I started keeping one of my own.

There are any number of animals I have fallen in love with and determined to bring home. I've adopted five cats — and with apologies to cat lovers round the world — they each lasted less than a week once I discovered how wonderful cats aren't, at least when compared to my faithful dogs. Cats climbing up the laundry rack, their claws shredding clean clothing; cats clawing their way up silk curtains; and most criminal of all — cats harassing my endlessly adoring collies.

"No," the collies informed me. "Just no."

Other animals have similarly wormed their way into my heart, with heavy emphasis on cows. Not that I live on a farm, but there is something soul-stirring in the liquid depths of those brown eyes. Those calf eyes beg me to bring them home and let them munch the lawn.

Once again, sanity, driven by the resignation that the collies own the lawn, that the calf will evolve into a large cow with hooves to kick the dogs, has prevailed every time I've considered bringing home a baby calf.

But of all the creatures I have encountered, betta fish have failed to move me.

I'm not saying I don't like fish in a tank. They're beautiful to watch, their swimming graceful and seemingly effortless, gliding through a physical property which, when torrents are unleashed, wreaks havoc on anything in its path. I've marveled at fish, the way they can breathe underwater, their smooth silence, their aloof superiority. In that, I've always believed fish were even more aloof than cats.

Up till now.

Last September, when my daughter Isabelle left, I adopted her fish. It took three weeks before I remembered it existed. When I did recall that she'd kept a blue betta in a bowl, my reaction was one of horror.

Three weeks without food in a half gallon of water that hadn't been changed. Whether I like fish or not, I owed it to the poor creature to give it a decent flushing, at the least.

I drummed up the courage to go to Isabelle's apartment to determine Charlie's status. Although we hadn't talked much recently about the pros and cons of this fish, I did remember the betta's name. I'm not sure why she decided upon it — knowing Isabelle, it was probably a joke about tuna, i.e. "Sorry, Charlie," channeling the Beatnik tuna mascot StarKist used for decades to pitch its canned fish.

As it was, I didn't have much hope for Charlie being alive, so I figured it didn't matter if I couldn't recall his name.

Walking into her apartment, I tried to remember where he was. In Isabelle's previous place, she'd kept several fish (spaced out between inevitable deaths) in a small tank on her desk that overlooked the street. It had faced west, with lots of sunshine. We'd both discussed the beneficence of giving a fish an opportunity to look out the window and enjoy the light play on the leaves of the tree outside the window. Not that we were sure fish did this. Options are nice, though.

I walked into her new apartment led by my nose. I was damned sure the fish was dead — after three weeks, the thing had to smell, right?

I discovered Charlie in his small plastic bowl on Isabelle's dresser in the bedroom. He was floating and it wasn't sideways. Nearly motionless, the betta seemed tiny and deflated, hanging on for whatever purpose it found it worthwhile. I scooped up the little bowl and the container of betta pellets and set it gently on the passenger seat in my car. I could flush him at home.

But the betta fish wasn't dead. The thing had an immense will to live.

Charlie was fed and his water changed. He gazed listlessly at the brown pellets, but managed to float to the water's surface. Opening his mouth, and with an intake of breath that seemed to encompass a sigh, he sucked in one or two of them.

Intrigued, I spent the next several hours reading everything I could find about betta fish. What they ate and when, the best size tank to keep them in. Morbidly, I read horror stories of fish deaths: bettas that had jumped out of bowls to land on the floor, only to be scraped off with a spatula hours later — nearly dried out, but still a fish. I read how bettas, bred as Siamese fighting fish, hated tank mates, hated a water current, and were susceptible to all manner of fish ailments. A betta might bite the fins or fight with any but the most docile fish in its tank, comments warned on fish sites.

And yet, as is most often true, there were exceptions. So I began to experiment.

The next day I bought Charlie (who I decided to rename 'Fishy' in case I became too attached to my new, blue friend) a two-gallon tank with a number of artificial plants. After a week of hard, brown pellets, I bought him flakes, then expanded the feeding program by adding dried shrimp to be crumbled enticingly across the water's top.

Fishy re-inflated. He swam round and round the tank. Even more miraculously, he knew when it was feeding time. Swimming to the front of the tank, Fishy waggled his fins and tail (in opposite directions all at once), opening and shutting his mouth, begging for food.

He was no different from a dog, except he didn't bark. And as an old lawyers' proverb goes, 'The fish got hooked because it opened its mouth.'

Except in this instance, I was the one who'd been hooked, fallen hook, line, and sinker for this silent yet engaging blue creature.

Off to the fish store I went. I'd read that Fishy really wanted to eat minuscule blood worms. Every morning. Scrumptious.

He sucked them down like spaghetti, chasing a cascade of worms to the bottom of the tank, scavenging among the rocks for half an hour each morning to make sure he hadn't missed one.

The collies were wary. They sensed I was cheating on them, feeding Fishy before them each morning. To their minds, it was beyond cheeky.

Ignoring them, I bought a bigger tank and added tank mates. Along the way, Fishy's name changed once more. And our conversations saw a change in tone.

Big Blue Terror: *I get that you bought three Otocinclus to clean up the mess I've made (algae). But man are they skittish (he whined while going nose-to-nose with the largest Oto.)*

Me: *Back off the Otos, you big blue terror.*

Big Blue Terror: *Just curious. Nothing more. But these panda corys, geez. Darting, scampering. No dignity whatsoever.*

Me: *Play nice. You looked bored in there. You can only sleep so much.*

The other morning, the panda corys discovered the fish feast of bloodworms and I watched in trepidation. Would this be the time when the big blue terror gave them the thrashing he believed they deserved?

Nearly tripping over each other to find food, they fed alongside Big Blue. Swimming beneath and through Blue's flowing fins, they swam circles around him. He remained nonplussed.

I sense he is looking at me with amusement at their antics. "These kids," he says. "You can't get any respect."

He sounds like he's channeling the jiving Charlie the Tuna. Maybe Isabelle knew something when she named him, all those months ago.

Off he swims, in search of food, in search of a quiet spot near the top of the tank amongst the artificial greenery. Until he decides it's time to mingle again.

TALES RETOLD: MARGARET MITCHELL, MICHELANGELO, AND AUNT JEMIMA

JULY 24, 2020

Statues and novels are methods of storytelling, each capturing a snapshot in time. While conveying a point of view, they also offer a contemporary source for learning about history.

Today's heated rhetoric fanning the flames of the culture war over removing Confederate statues, along with other statues perceived to project a racially divisive slant, brings to mind two of my favorite books when I was growing up.

From the Mixed-Up Files of Mrs. Basil E. Frankweiler and *Gone with the Wind* are stories that helped enlarge my worldview. Each is a classic in its own right; each a story about fabulous places, and what drives human nature.

After reading these books multiple times over, I have a sense of how my personality developed. Whether the stories had something to do with that, I'm not certain. But fiction which touches on history wrapped up in good storytelling can instill a lifelong interest in pursuing the truth.

E. L. Konigsburg's *From the Mixed-Up Files of Mrs. Basil E. Frankweiler* is a Newbery Medal winning children's book about a sister and brother who run away from their home in Connecticut to New York City. They spend a week living in the Metropolitan Museum of Art. Running away from home when you're a sixth-grade girl is a trope reserved for an age of burgeoning adulthood. But it's where Claudia and Jamie run away to that gives the story its novelty. Who hasn't dreamt of living in a grand museum unnoticed by grownups? Not to mention sleeping in the antique beds of queens and bathing in public fountains?

There is certainly untapped potential for adventure with this plot formula. Contemporary riffs on the idea — the 2006 movie, *Night at the Museum,* and overnight programs where you can explore under the watchful eyes of museum docents masquerading as camp counselors — come to mind.

The *Mixed-Up Files'* story focuses on a beautiful marble angel statue with an enigmatic provenance. The plot centers on whether Angel was the work of the Italian sculptor, Michelangelo. The book sparked my interest in the famed artist. At thirteen, when my grandma invited me on a trip to Europe — a trip whose itinerary I could design — any city where I could see Michelangelo's art was fair game. My goal was to find Michelangelo's mysterious Angel.

In actuality, the statue was a work of fiction.

In all my museum wanderings since then, I have marveled at the David and Pieta but have never encountered a Michelangelo 'Angel' statue. I have earned a crick in my neck from too much gazing upwards at the Vatican's heavenly Sistine Chapel ceiling. While gawking at its detailed figures, I have also learned how the ceiling is a canvas Michelangelo 'embedded with subversive messages in his spectacular frescoes — not only Jewish, Kabbalistic and pagan symbols but also insults directed at Pope Julius II, who commissioned the work, and references to Michelangelo's own sexuality.' [2]

It seems, then, that Michelangelo and his art contain stories within the story. Only after some research and contemplation might they be deciphered.

I've similarly searched for Margaret Mitchell and her genteel antebellum Atlanta on several trips there. I know the Civil War epic inside and out. Channeling Scarlett O'Hara as a teenager, my friend Kim and I used to sit for hours in either of our bedrooms — and

---

[2]Drake, Cathryn, "Did Michelangelo Have a Hidden Agenda?" The Wall Street Journal, November 14, 2008, https://www.wsj.com/articles/SB122661765227326251

if shooed outside by parents, you would find us reading lines from GWTW while perched on Kim's trampoline. Kim took on all the characters save one: she read Mammy, Rhett Butler, Melanie Wilkes, and Ashley. I reserved Scarlett for myself. My justification was slim. I was a green-eyed brunette, Kim a curly blonde. Mostly, Kim put up with me, I think in part because I let her read the part of *Little Women's* Amy, who got to marry Laurie, after all.

From our repeated readings of the story, and backed up by the floridly technicolor movie, Kim and I, along with the rest of the world, developed a rosy impression of the antebellum South and the war that ripped through it, leaving Confederate society and their well-cared for slaves in tatters, a cause lost.

As I grew up and read more history, I learned how the Lost Cause of the Confederacy became a mythology tangled around a premise of human enslavement.

The fact that nearly four million people were part and parcel of an economic system designed to ensure white supremacy was a subtext of GWTW that I finally understood. It was there in Ashley's late-night political meetings; it was spelled out in the childlike submissiveness of Tara's slaves. And it was accentuated by the outrageous single-minded purpose of Southern belles who graced the porches and porticos of every antebellum home.

The South that had been lost was glorified by the United Daughters of the Confederacy and others, in songs, stories, and statues so well-meaning it was hard to not believe the intentions — no matter how violent or oppressive — were for a common good.

Margaret Mitchell, or Peggy, as she called herself, grew up a debutante in the early 1900s, wrapped in tales of this golden world, mostly through the eyes of her family and friends. Reputed to be a virtuoso flirt, she most likely was her own model for the novel's forthright heroine.

In reality, after annulling her three-month marriage, Mitchell married John Marsh, her first husband's best man. They turned down an offer to live in her father's mansion, preferring instead Apartment One, 979 Crescent Avenue, with rooms totaling 650 square feet. Mitchell referred to that home as 'The Dump', a place where she hosted Prohibition-era parties with bootleg liquor and dressed as a flapper. A former features writer for *The Atlanta Journal*

Sunday Magazine, she also enjoyed reading erotica. It was there on Crescent Avenue that she wrote her venerated historical novel.

Given Mitchell's backstory, she might have had an agenda in telling the over-the-top tale of *Gone with the Wind.*

Writing about Scarlett's shenanigans, the repeated occurrences of embarrassing family and friends with unseemly actions — from dancing in public while in mourning to running a lumber mill, all while bouncing from husband to husband — it's occurred to some that Mitchell's goal was to present a counterpoint to the South's glorious past. That in creating a heroine like Scarlett, she was setting women free from their society's enslavement.

And then there is Aunt Jemima. Subsequent to recent Black Lives Matter protests prompted by the murder of George Floyd on May 26, 2020, Quaker Foods decided to change the name and logo of its pancake mix and syrup. Aunt Jemima was a figurative character, portrayed by Nancy Green, a black cook recruited in 1890 to play a pancake queen born into slavery and freed to be a housekeeper and nanny. Promotional materials created the mythical character with a back story that included saving her Mississippi plantation owner's mustache. It's pancakes, remember? They didn't want it to get too gory.

The Aunt Jemima icon isn't a tangible statue, but instead a portrayal of the human form serving to objectify a racial stereotype. But the Mammy caricatures upon which it's modeled are well known. Aunt Jemina's story is another example of whitewashing Confederate history.

All this makes me think of statues I've seen in museums over the years.

The ones from ancient Greece and Rome, alongside statues pillaged from other countries that are now housed at the British Museum. Statues with their heads lopped off pepper Europe, and there are statues of Catholic missionaries in Santa Fe, New Mexico, a stone portrayal of people who committed mass genocide with the church's approval.

These stories and statues represent one point of view, through the eyes of those who commissioned the works, or more likely, through the artistry of the storyteller.

Times change and with them the temperature, a barometer of society and what is relevant now. If we took down statues that are deemed racially divisive today and displayed them in a way that contextualizes the backstory, we can learn America's mottled history.

Margaret Mitchell put it this way:

'I was never one to patiently pick up broken fragments and glue them together again and tell myself that the mended whole was as good as new. What is broken is broken – and I'd rather remember it as it was at its best than mend it and see the broken places as long as I lived.' [3]

History is written by the winners. When ideologies change, the way the past is portrayed always gets a fresh take. What's broken will always stay broken. It's up to us to understand it in the light of history.

---

[3]Margaret Mitchell Quotes. BrainyQuote.com, BrainyMedia Inc, 2021. https://www.brainyquote.com/quotes/margaret_mitchell_157606, accessed February 6, 2021.

THE YEAR THAT GLITTERED

DECEMBER 31, 2020

The year 2020 illuminated the true nature of so much. It was a year of everything, and throughout it, the year never stopped glittering.

My eighty-two-year-old mother insists that 2020 was the year that wasn't. But since she is all too accustomed to me disagreeing with her about many things, the fact we have diverse opinions on this topic isn't earth-shattering. Because in my experience, as far as happenings go, the year of the coronavirus pandemic was like no other.

It was a year of everything, and throughout its twelve months, the year never stopped glittering. For nine months now, there have been heart-stopping moments where we waited, counting days, deaths, and the number of open hospital beds left to fill with patients, who when stricken with this novel virus, cannot breathe.

In this time, I have noticed that an object can be iridescent only when diffracted light shines on it. Without light, its glitter remains hidden in murky darkness. In that, things can only glitter when light reveals their true nature.

In the year 2020, glitter exposed discord and disfunction. We anticipated an election that would put an end to a malignant presidential administration, one serving only the man in the Oval Office. We endured an election cycle that seemingly had no end. Horrified, we watched the president use frivolous lawsuits, arm-twisting, and threats to elected officials, judges, and citizens, attempting to invalidate election results once he proved soundly defeated. An attempt at a presidential coup d'état — however seditious, however poorly executed — and a possibility duly addressed by our country's founders when crafting the Constitution, is not a mainstream occurrence in the annals of the United States.

In the midst of partisan warring, so extreme the likes of which has not been seen for 150 years, there was social unrest. People protested racial injustice on the heels of the George Floyd and Breonna Taylor murders — and so many, many more black lives lost at the hands of unscrupulous police.

Close to home, we watched our world burn. Orange smoke suffocated Colorado's bluebird ceiling, with thick black ash of incinerated forests drifting onto porches and lawn furniture all summer long and into the fall. Because of the fires, staying at home and abiding by mandated state orders became all that much less palatable. Before the fires started in mid-August — the Cameron Peak Fire being the first of a set — we could at least escape for a few hours to cycle county roads and wish we were cycling anyplace else but here.

There were so many things we experienced at every twist and turn in 2020 that with each next permutation of unlikely combinations, we wondered what more of everything could be left.

And the glitter never stopped flowing from our emotional faucets.

There was so much of everything that we wished we could have more of nothing. The mundane, the quotidian, the normality — oh, how much we missed it.

In that, 2020 was a year of blinders off. Stripped bare of frills and accessories, living was simplified, with expectations and priorities realigned. A near-constant firehose of information exacerbated the stress and uncertainty of what was the right way to proceed — that if we took the wrong action, we might usher in disease, death, and economic frailty. There were periods of frenzy, which when tempered by repetition, became dulled into familiarity, until once again, the drumbeat of the media harvested yet another topic for us to latch onto, promoting a steadily roiling landscape of panicky moments.

In this year of nothing that was everything, I learned that fish in a tank glitter in water, but only while they are alive, and only when their LED aquarium lighting is on. My collie puppies' fur glitters effortlessly in sunlight, while my aged dogs' coats have become dull and lackluster, no matter how much brushing I bestow. Tears glitter, too, whether induced by anger or fear, joy and love, longing, loneliness, or loss. Tears are shed from hopelessness, too. Those tears glitter no differently from other tears, yet as they are mostly experienced when we are alone, are they tears we can see?

There are glittering falsehoods and fables spun by our elected leaders, and then there is the glitter of madness.

Our daughter Isabelle, diagnosed with bipolar disorder at 19, struggled to accept her illness for years. We struggled alongside her, mourning the loss, missing the shining star she had been. A high school valedictorian, mental illness robbed Isabelle of her self-assurance and drive. Medications clouded her mind and stole her creativity. Sluggish and unenthusiastic about what seemed a death sentence for a promising future, as do many who struggle with a mind out of control, she resorted to alcohol to ease her pain. At age twenty-five, she gave up, determined to live without medication — and to just be.

Her mind tormented and psychotic, she left us, spending time in a psychiatric hospital, and on release, becoming homeless for five months. When she reached out to us on March 19, Colorado was ten days into phase one of what would be an ever-changing landscape of business and school shutdowns. Isabelle wanted to come home.

I first saw a COVID-19 meme on a video, one depicting huge, spiked inflatables rolling down empty city streets and scaling building exteriors. Next came the blurred, spiky fuzz ball, looking much like one of my dryer lint balls studded with red velour sock shrapnel.

In the early lockdown days, I divided my time between panic scrolling about the mess the world had gotten itself into — reading every science article I could to understand something, anything, about this new virus that had popped up in Wuhan, China — and devouring articles on how to manage and treat psychosis.

My husband, Dr. K, an oncologist for 29 years, found himself transitioning backwards to his residency days, wearing surgical scrubs to treat his clinic patients, returning home to strip down to underwear in the garage lest his clothing infect Isabelle and me as he headed to the shower. He labeled our situation succinctly. It was an intersection of two tornadoes.

Experiencing life in lockdown differed for everyone.

Friends spent the first month or so of the shutdowns frantically sourcing hand sanitizer and Clorox wipes because the Centers for Disease Control weren't sure how long the virus lived on surfaces. I cleaned haphazardly, wiping down door knobs, my cell phone, and scrupulously sterilizing kitchen counter tops, knowing it to be a fruitless task. Isabelle was certain she had discovered the cure to COVID, and talking to herself in an endless monotone, she carried on conversations with people who didn't exist. When the voices she heard didn't agree with her, she yelled at them.

Friends posted on Facebook how their days were quiet. Boredom threatened to overtake their lives. The schools closed, restaurants were shuttered by the Colorado Department of Public Health and Environment, and businesses offered curbside pickup.

When people were first ordered to stay in their houses, there were toilet paper and grocery shortages. As state health departments cautiously began reopening society, masks became the next must-have item. With PPE — personal protection equipment — scarce and reserved for those on the healthcare front lines, home-sewn masks proliferated, with people trying to outdo one another in numbers sewn.

We cancelled one vacation after another — a visit to Harrison and his wife, Alex, in Atlanta; a bike trip to Santa Fe; the June trip to Atlanta, rescheduled on the off-chance that this pandemic thing was simply hype and would fade away. The bicycling trip to Prague? That got cancelled, too.

Through it all, during those days, Isabelle ranted. She screamed. She disappeared on long walks late into the night during which we were frantic — would she come home, or worse — in a skewed perception of priorities, would she contract the virus and infect us?

In early April, in tandem with millions, we Zoomed with friends, never letting on that Isabelle had returned. She needed protection, if not from us, then from herself.

On Zoom, millions of pixels on the computer screen glittered, capturing our images into tiny squares. There was no talking at once, no cacophony of excitement, no heated conversations. We longed for tactile touches but knew those could infect us.

Quiet times brought opportunities for healing. As spring turned to summer, Isabelle's willingness to talk with her psychiatrist and therapist on virtual visits began to bear fruit. The doctor, using the tried-and-true method of trial-and-error, slowly encouraged her, with us alongside, into taking a pharmaceutical cocktail that might bring the return of the Isabelle we knew.

In that, Isabelle's madness stopped glittering. The daughter I remembered from years past re-emerged, damaged, but determined to heal. There was a glimmer of hope.

Summer of 2020 saw socially distanced cocktail patio parties with our Zoom COVID bubble, the one highly anticipated activity on Saturday night replacing what had been an often hectic pre-pandemic social schedule. Five couples and Isabelle, each sitting in BYO lawn chairs, wearing masks, never touching, no hugs allowed. We cheered on Isabelle's return to sanity. And we cheered on the healthcare heroes guided by Dr. Anthony Fauci's steadfast assurances that we could get through this.

If only.

If only we followed the guidelines, wore the masks, shut the businesses, closed the schools, and prevented restaurants from serving too many people indoors. The dos and don'ts of the list were overwhelming, and not all chose to comply. Masks became a visible banner of a culture war, one that had been brewing for decades. In bubbling to the surface, treading on bleak, unfamiliar ground, we came to see people for who they truly were.

This virus has done more than damage our lungs and kill nearly 300,000 Americans as I write. The pandemic ripped off the facade of our civilization. The masks we wear hide more than our breath, breath that kills others. They mask hatred for the other, the different, the opposition. Those who refuse to mask, believing it weak, show their scorn for those who do all that more willingly. The virus has stripped us of caring, kindness, and reason when it doesn't fit the confines of our belief systems.

But tellingly, the year has also been filled with pockets of peaceful silence. Is this nature's way of telling us that we needed to slow down? That life in the year 2020 is too complicated, too fast, too much? That we needed to step back for introspection, to solve problems at home in our families, our communities, our country?

Many will dispute me on this. The damage to the economy, they'll cry. The lives lost. No, those permanent scars did not have to happen, if common sense and public health policy, learned from pandemics and communal disease suffered by societies past, had some effect on our actions. If people had listened to those who came before us.

I pull a greeting card from its box to enclose with a Hanukkah gift I'll mail to Harrison and Alex. If we are lucky, if the vaccine rollout stays on schedule, we might see them next summer. It will be nearly two years since we've last hugged.

A cloud of glitter comes out of the card box, falling on my lap, my desk, the floor. The glitter is green. It is an ever-present reminder of the things that didn't happen this year, and the too many things that did. But as a reminder that love is evergreen, it offers an opportunity for reflections on the possibility of peace.